DISEASES & DISORDERS

Depression

Lydia D. Bjornlund

LUCENT BOOKS
A part of Gale, Cengage Learning

GALE
CENGAGE Learning™

Detroit • New York • San Francisco • New Haven, Conn • Waterville, Maine • London

LIBRARY OF CONGRESS CATALOGING-IN-PUBLICATION DATA

Bjornlund, Lydia D.
  Depression / by Lydia Bjornlund.
    p. cm. -- (Diseases & disorders)
  Includes bibliographical references and index.
  ISBN 978-1-4205-0217-6 (hardcover)
  1. Depression, Mental--Popular works. I. Title.
  RC537.B515 2010
  616.85'27--dc22

                                                    2009033487

Lucent Books
27500 Drake Rd.
Farmington Hills, MI 48331

ISBN-13: 978-1-4205-0217-6
ISBN-10: 1-4205-0217-4

Printed in the United States of America
1 2 3 4 5 6 7 14 13 12 11 10
Printed by Bang Printing, Brainerd, MN, 1st Ptg., 02/2010

Table of Contents

"The Most Difficult Puzzles Ever Devised"

Charles Best, one of the pioneers in the search for a cure for diabetes, once explained what it is about medical research that intrigued him so. "It's not just the gratification of knowing one is helping people," he confided, "although that probably is a more heroic and selfless motivation. Those feelings may enter in, but truly, what I find best is the feeling of going toe to toe with nature, of trying to solve the most difficult puzzles ever devised. The answers are there somewhere, those keys that will solve the puzzle and make the patient well. But how will those keys be found?"

Since the dawn of civilization, nothing has so puzzled people—and often frightened them, as well—as the onset of illness in a body or mind that had seemed healthy before. A seizure, the inability of a heart to pump, the sudden deterioration of muscle tone in a small child—being unable to reverse such conditions or even to understand why they occur was unspeakably frustrating to healers. Even before there were names for such conditions, even before they were understood at all, each was a reminder of how complex the human body was, and how vulnerable.

While our grappling with understanding diseases has been frustrating at times, it has also provided some of humankind's most heroic accomplishments. Alexander Fleming's accidental discovery in 1928 of a mold that could be turned into penicillin has resulted in the saving of untold millions of lives. The isolation of the enzyme insulin has reversed what was once a death sentence for anyone with diabetes. There have been great strides in combating conditions for which there is not yet a cure, too. Medicines can help AIDS patients live longer, diagnostic tools such as mammography and ultrasounds can help doctors find tumors while they are treatable, and laser surgery techniques have made the most intricate, minute operations routine.

This "toe-to-toe" competition with diseases and disorders is even more remarkable when seen in a historical continuum. An astonishing amount of progress has been made in a very short time. Just two hundred years ago, the existence of germs as a cause of some diseases was unknown. In fact, it was less than 150 years ago that a British surgeon named Joseph Lister had difficulty persuading his fellow doctors that washing their hands before delivering a baby might increase the chances of a healthy delivery (especially if they had just attended to a diseased patient)!

Each book in Lucent's Diseases and Disorders series explores a disease or disorder and the knowledge that has been accumulated (or discarded) by doctors through the years. Each book also examines the tools used for pinpointing a diagnosis, as well as the various means that are used to treat or cure a disease. Finally, new ideas are presented—techniques or medicines that may be on the horizon.

Frustration and disappointment are still part of medicine, for not every disease or condition can be cured or prevented. But the limitations of knowledge are being pushed outward constantly; the "most difficult puzzles ever devised" are finding challengers every day.

INTRODUCTION

Beyond Sadness

Everyone occasionally feels blue or sad, but these feelings usually pass within a few hours. Even when dealing with grief or a major sorrow, people typically begin to feel a bit better in a few days. Those suffering from depression, on the other hand, may not be able to identify a reason for their sadness. In contrast to normal feelings of sadness, depression is a more generalized and persistent feeling of gloom or despair that can significantly interfere with a person's thoughts, mood, behavior, and physical health.

A depressive disorder interferes with daily life and causes pain for both the person with the disorder and those who care about him or her. One woman diagnosed with depression describes how it saps her energy:

> The things with depression that bother me the most are feeling like you're encased in cement, where you just can't drag your body out of bed, where the simplest of tasks is just daunting and you have to force yourself to re-focus and to pick yourself up and to take that shower, get to the grocery store, get the kids off to school, get to the office, get through your day.[1]

Depression is a common but serious illness that affects more than 100 million people worldwide. According to the National Institute of Mental Health (NIMH), about 19 million Americans—9.5 percent of the population—suffer from depression. Fortunately, the vast majority of people—even those with severe depression—can get better with treatment.

Depression has always existed, but its causes have never been fully understood. Many years ago, people believed that mental illnesses, including depression—or melancholia, as it was called then—were the result of an imbalance in bodily fluids. People also once thought mental illness was a sign of the devil. Throughout history, depression has also been viewed as a lack of willpower, laziness, or simply a disagreeable nature.

Today, depression is viewed as having both situational and physical causes. While most experts agree that depression is a serious mental illness, many people worry that natural, and in many cases, appropriate, feelings of sadness or grief may be misdiagnosed as a "disease." Depression is different from grief or loneliness. When people are grieving, they mourn their loss but retain a sense of self-esteem. Lonely people may be

People suffering from depression experience persistent feelings of melancholy and hopelessness.

sad, but they do not have an impending sense of dread that is associated with depression.

Many patients who suffer from depression say they cannot live without the drugs and therapy they receive as part of their treatment plan. "Every morning I wake up and dread getting out of bed," says Bernard, an eighty-three-year-old who was diagnosed with depression five years ago. "But after I have my [antidepressant] pill, I always feel much better."[2]

Depression is a mental illness that affects millions of people in countless ways. Some people are able to continue going to school, to their jobs, to the many other activities that they enjoy. But for many, depression is a debilitating disease that stops them in their tracks. They find it difficult to get out of bed or to take care of themselves, let alone their family. They feel a sense of hopelessness. The good news is that depression can be treated. Even for the most severe cases of depression, proper diagnosis and treatment can lead to long, healthy, and productive lives.

CHAPTER ONE

What Is Depression?

At times, we all feel sad in response to a loss, disappointment, or frustration. This is normal. Many people who are sad say they are "depressed," but sadness in response to a specific situation is normal. Clinical depression is vastly different from these temporary states. Unlike normal feelings of sadness, depression overwhelms a person, lasts a long time, and interferes with his or her day-to-day life.

Some people describe depression as a black hole or a curtain coming down over their life. People suffering from depression often see no hope. They may have a constant feeling of impending doom. In fact, some people with depression do not feel sad as much as lifeless or empty. They may be unable to experience any emotions at all.

How Serious Is Depression?

A recent study sponsored by the World Health Organization and the World Bank found major depression to be the fourth leading cause of disability worldwide, and it is anticipated to become the second most disabling disease by 2020 (surpassed only by heart disease). The National Alliance on Mental Illness says that major depression is the leading cause of disability in the United States and many other developed countries.

One reason for the level of disability is the sheer duration of depressive episodes. A major study of patients who required hospitalization for depression found that the median time to

Symptoms of Depression

Symptoms vary from one person to another and may change over time. The symptoms typically associated with depression include:
- persistent feelings of sadness or anxiety
- irritability or restlessness
- decreased interest or pleasure in hobbies and activities (called anhedonia)
- loss of energy; tiredness
- overeating or loss of appetite
- weight loss or weight gain
- insomnia, difficulty sleeping, early morning awakening, or sleeping too much
- inability to concentrate; memory loss
- indecisiveness
- pessimism
- feelings of worthlessness, hopelessness, or guilt
- persistent aches or pains, cramps, or digestive problems that do not ease with treatment
- thoughts of suicide or death

recover was five months. In other words, half of the people hospitalized for depression recovered in five months or less; the other half needed longer than five months. Another problem is that many people have recurring incidences of depression or continue to experience some residual symptoms of depression even after they are feeling better.

Depression is classified as a mood disorder, a term used for any disorder in which a disturbance in the person's mood is the main feature or problem. One of the most common and most serious types of depression is major depression, which is also called major depressive disorder or clinical depression. Other types of depression include dysthymia, seasonal affective disorder, and postpartum depression. These types of depression vary greatly in onset and severity.

Major Depression

Major depression, the most severe type of depression, affects roughly 14.8 million American adults—or 5 to 8 percent of the population—in any given year. People young and old suffer from clinical depression; the median age for onset is thirty-two years. People who have gone through an episode of depression are at risk of having another episode at one point or another. Some people experience recurring episodes of major depression throughout their lives.

Major depression prevents a person from functioning normally. It is characterized by a combination of symptoms that interfere with a person's ability to work, study, sleep, and eat. The signs and symptoms vary from one person to another. Many depressed people complain that they have no energy. They may be constantly anxious or irritable. Concentration and memory problems are common, making tasks more difficult. People may not have energy to do much of anything; activities that were once fun are no longer enjoyable. Some people have difficulty sleeping or staying asleep; others sleep all the time. Some individuals lose their appetite, while others eat constantly to fill the void they feel in their lives. Often, people with major depression have little sense of self-worth and an overwhelming sense of dread or hopelessness.

Some people struggle with major depressive episodes all their lives. Singer Sheryl Crow, for instance, has said that she has experienced chronic depression since she was a child. During one six-month period in the late 1980s, there were days when Crow's depression made it impossible for her to leave the house: "During some of those darkest days, I'd hardly get out of bed and just let the phone ring and ring. Small problems became insurmountable." Still, like many of those who suffer from major depression, Crow was helped through antidepressants and psychotherapy. "For some reason, surrounded by

Famed singer Sheryl Crow, who has struggled with depression throughout her life, has learned to cope with the illness.

my friends on my [fortieth] birthday, it was like there was a sudden break in the clouds. Depression goes away as suddenly as it descends."[3]

Dysthymia

Dysthymia, also called dysthymic disorder, is a relatively common form of depression. The word *dysthymia* comes from the Greek term meaning "ill humor or bad mood." Dysthymia is a chronic form of depression that affects 5 to 6 percent of the U.S. population.

The symptoms of dysthymia are less severe than in episodes of major depressive disorder. Life is gray and uninteresting.

People with dysthymia feel mildly depressed on most days over a period of at least two years. Studies show that dysthymia usually has a gradual onset, often in people in their late teens or early twenties with a family history of depression. People who are socially isolated or who lack strong support groups are particularly vulnerable.

Although its symptoms are less debilitating, dysthymia is a serious form of depression. It rarely goes away without being treated with drugs or psychotherapy or a combination of both. Dysthymia can occur alone or with more severe depression. In one study, 76 percent of people with dysthymia had a major depressive episode within five years of diagnosis.

In *Depression and Bipolar Disorder* psychiatrist Virginia Edwards describes Martin, a hardworking executive who suffers from dysthymia. Martin is somewhat difficult to get along with at work, but he is a valued employee because he runs the office efficiently. Like many people with dysthymia, Martin rarely goes out socially. He tends to find fault with his friends and the women to whom he is introduced. "Martin can't remember a time when he felt relaxed and happy," Edwards writes. "He is always anticipating trouble and worried about the future. He thinks other people must feel the same way but manage to hide it better."[4]

Seasonal Affective Disorder

Several other depression-related mood disorders are triggered by specific aspects of a person's environment. Seasonal affective disorder (SAD), for instance, is characterized by the depressive episodes that occur only during the winter months, when there is less sunlight. Differences in mood are common ailments: People often talk of the "winter blues" or "cabin fever" they get when cooped up all winter. SAD is typically diagnosed when these mood changes are severe and when they occur over two or more seasons. Although SAD is usually considered a "winter" disease, a rarer form of the disorder affects people during the summer months.

Fantasy writer Barbara Hambly says she first noticed symptoms of depression when she took a trip to Australia at the age of fifteen. "My memories of Australia are a bit ambiguous, because I suffer from seasonal affective disorder: depression in the winter as the hours of sunlight shorten," Hambly writes. "It took me until I was nearly fifty to figure it out, but the equatorial swap from midsummer to midwinter causes a dislocation in my brain-chemistry whose effect is to throw me into severe depression—exacerbated by whatever else is going on in my life or in the world at the time."[5]

SAD has been linked to a biochemical imbalance in the brain prompted by less daylight. Sufferers experience many of the

Seasonal affective disorder (SAD) is a depressed state occurring only during the dreary winter months.

same symptoms as with major depression, but the SAD patient almost always has an increase in sleep, complaining of chronic fatigue throughout the winter months. In addition, an increase in appetite rather than a decrease is more common; SAD patients may gain weight each winter. Many SAD sufferers report food cravings, particularly for sweets and carbohydrates. With SAD, these symptoms go away during the spring and summer months. Approximately 500,000 American adults seek treatment for SAD each year. The incidence appears to be higher among women than men.

Postpartum Depression

Another common situational type of depression is postpartum depression. This term is used to describe a major depressive episode experienced by a mother after having a baby. Postpartum depression usually occurs in the first few weeks, but for some women the onset may come several months after delivery. In addition to changes in hormone levels, experts cite sleep deprivation, increased stress that comes from having to care for a baby, and a loss of the sense of self and control over one's self as contributing factors to postpartum depression.

In *Down Came the Rain,* actress Brook Shields describes her depression following the birth of her baby: "I was in a bizarre state of mind, experiencing feelings that ranged from embarrassment to stoicism to melancholy to shock, practically at once. I didn't feel at all joyful."[6] Shields assumed she would bounce back when she had gotten enough rest from her difficult labor, but her feelings intensified: "During what was becoming one of the darkest points in my life, I sat holding my newborn and could not avoid the image of her flying through the air and hitting the wall in front of me."[7] Shields worried that the feelings showed no signs of letting up. "This felt like my life was over and I would never be happy again."[8]

Postpartum depression is estimated to affect 10 to 15 percent of new mothers. Women who experience postpartum depression after one birth are more likely to have a recurring episode after subsequent births. The symptoms are the same

After childbirth some women experience postpartum depression, which may interfere with a new mother's ability to care for her newborn.

as with any major depressive episode, but postpartum depression can interfere with the mother's ability to care for and bond with her newborn.

Psychotic Depression

In some cases, depression becomes so severe that the sufferers develop delusions or hallucinations. They might think they are already dead or that they are responsible for war, hunger, or natural disaster. They might hear voices saying they are worthless or urging suicide or other destructive behavior. When people become out of touch with reality, they are said to be suffering from psychotic depression. In *Psychotic Depression*, Conrad Schwartz and Edward Shorter describe a woman diagnosed with psychotic depression:

> [She had been] talking to the television, stating delusions that her husband is a famous religious icon, threatening him, and battering him. She was unkempt, quiet, and emotionally flat, and she moved little. She spoke slowly, answered "I don't know" to most questions, and reported hearing the voice of a holy man and seeing people who were not there.[9]

Psychotic depression is more common among elderly people. It tends to strike less healthy people who have a history of psychosis and depression in their family. Relatively rare, this is a serious form of depression because people may give in to the voices that haunt them. Images of brains of patients with this form of depression suggest that the disease may be due to a brain abnormality. Most people suffering from psychotic depression do not recover without treatment.

Depression and Bipolar Disorder

Major depression, dysthymia, SAD, and psychotic depression are all characterized by intense lows. These forms of depression are sometimes called unipolar depression to differentiate them from bipolar disorder, a mood disorder in which the lows are interspersed with highs. Sometimes people can swing rapidly between moods, but usually the change from one mood to another is fairly gradual. One sufferer describes the symptoms:

> If you have bipolar [disorder] as I do, . . . you wear many faces. You are either the life of the party and feel that life is wonderful and so much fun, only to wake up the next day so depressed you think you won't make it until the next day. Then within a few hours or 6 months, you are screaming at the top of your voice, feeling extremely out of control, extremely irritable and you want to smash everybody and everything around you.[10]

Roughly 5.5 million American adults have been diagnosed with bipolar disorder. Bipolar disorder differs from other forms of depression in both causes and treatments. Unlike unipolar depression, bipolar disorder almost always requires medical treatment for life.

Who Gets Depression?

Depression affects people from all walks of life. Many well-known people have suffered from major depression. It was once believed to be the curse of creative genius. Authors Hans

Christian Andersen, Ernest Hemingway, and J.K. Rowling are among the many authors who described their major depressive episodes. Dutch painter Vincent van Gogh also suffered from depression, probably from childhood. His sister said that as a child, Vincent was "intensely serious and uncommunicative, and walked around clumsily and in a daze, with his head hung low."[11] He himself later described his childhood as "gloomy and cold and sterile."[12] Abraham Lincoln also is believed to have been a lifelong sufferer of depression; major depressive episodes were exacerbated by the death of his son and the stress of the Civil War. British prime minister Winston Churchill also suffered from the disease, which he called his "black dog."

Lincoln and Churchill were in good company. A 2006 study by Duke University suggests that 24 percent of U.S. presidents suffered from depression. According to the study, at least ten

Nineteenth-century president Abraham Lincoln suffered from depression—intensified by his son's death and by the stress of the Civil War, which occurred during his presidency.

Famous People with Depression

Many famous people have been diagnosed with depression. J.K. Rowling recently discussed her depression and admitted that her despair was once so great she attempted suicide. Author Ann Rice also has discussed the depression she has suffered following the death of her husband. Like many others, Ernest Hemingway dealt with his depression through alcohol; Hemingway's grand-daughter Margaux, who became a famous actress, also suffered from severe depression—just one of the family connections that suggest a genetic factor. Contemporary musicians who have been diagnosed with depression include Janet Jackson, Elton John, Beyoncé Knowles, and Kurt Cobain, the lead singer of the highly successful band Nirvana, who committed suicide in 1994. Actors who have had major depressive episodes include Drew Barrymore, Kirsten Dunst, Gwyneth Paltrow, and Heath Ledger, who died of an overdose of prescription medications at the top of his career in 2008.

Depression does not strike only artistic temperaments. American astronaut Buzz Aldrin suffered from depression, as did Abraham Lincoln and Winston Churchill. In a 1995 interview Princess Diana revealed that she had suffered from postpartum depression after her first son, Prince William, was born. Singer Marie Osmond and actor Brooke Shields also have discussed their fight with postpartum depression following the birth of babies.

Of course, most people who suffer from depression are not famous. In fact, many cannot even hold down a job. Success can be difficult to achieve when even the simplest task seems like an immense hurdle. Many people with depression are successful in their fields only because they have succeeded first in obtaining an accurate diagnosis of and appropriate treatment for their illness.

presidents suffered from depressive episodes while in office. In almost all cases, the depressive symptoms interfered with their performance. Experts speculate that the stress of leading a nation may make national politicians particularly susceptible to depression.

Women and Depression

Women and men can both become depressed, but women are almost twice as likely to be diagnosed with depression. Experts believe women may be at higher risk due partly to hormonal changes brought on by puberty, menstruation, menopause, and pregnancy. Researchers have shown that hormones directly affect the parts of the brain that control mood. Many new mothers experience a brief episode of the "baby blues" immediately after giving birth; experts suggest that the depression that is sometimes diagnosed in new mothers—called postpartum depression—results from the same physical and emotional stresses as those causing more "normal" feelings. Studies also show that women who experience postpartum depression often have had prior depressive episodes and are more likely to experience major depression later in life.

Research suggests that hormonal changes may also account for depressive episodes during other times in a woman's life. The risk of depression increases with menopause, for instance. Scientists believe that the rise and fall of estrogen and other hormones may affect the brain chemistry that is associated with depressive illness.

Societal and environmental factors may also play a role. The stress of balancing work and home responsibilities, caring for young children and/or aging parents, abuse, poverty, and dealing with difficult relationships may all increase the risk of depression.

Men and Depression

The risk for depression is lower for men than for women, but men are by no means immune to the disorder. More than 6 million American men are treated for depression each year. Some experts suggest that the number of men with depression may actually be much higher because many men do not seek help. Although depression and other mental illnesses do not have the stigma they once did, many men still believe that asking for help for emotional problems is a sign of weakness.

Men also react to depressive feelings differently than women. Men are more likely to become hostile or violent. Others may turn to drugs or alcohol to deal with their feelings of despair or hopelessness. They may throw themselves into their work to avoid having to focus on their feelings, or engage in risky recreational pursuits, extreme sports, or reckless behavior. Suicide is an especially serious risk for men with depression. Although more women attempt suicide, men are four times more likely than women to succeed.

Depression in the Elderly

Depression among the elderly is sometimes difficult to diagnose. Seniors often have different, less obvious symptoms. They also may be less inclined to acknowledge feelings of sadness, and when they do, others may assume these feelings are normal for older people. As people age, they are more likely to experience the loss of loved ones. They may suddenly have to adjust to living alone after decades of living with a spouse or other family members. Older people also may suffer from pain. Even minor disabilities or illnesses, such as arthritis or diabetes, can interfere with the ability of a senior to enjoy life to the fullest. In addition, depression can be a side effect of some medications taken to treat such diseases.

Aging can be a stressful and anxious experience. Having to adjust to major life changes such as retirement or the transition into an assisted living community or a nursing home can contribute to the risk of depression. Retirees may no longer feel needed. Seniors may worry about getting sick or losing their mobility and their independence. Depression is often a secondary concern for those suffering from a chronic illness such as heart disease or cancer. Even healthy elderly people with depression may dwell on morbidity and have a fear of dying.

Elderly people may face a host of situations that can cause depression, such as the death of a spouse, chronic illness, and loneliness.

The changes people go through as they age can all contribute to depression, but it is important to note that depression is not a normal or necessary aspect of aging. In fact, studies show that most seniors are satisfied with their lives.

Depression can be hard to diagnose in elderly patients. Elderly people are more likely than younger adults to have a depressive illness that goes undetected and thus untreated, which may contribute to the high risk of suicide among older patients. Many people assume that the highest rates of suicide are among young people, but suicide is a problem among the elderly. Americans aged sixty-five and older account for about 13 percent of the population but almost 20 percent of all suicides. The suicide rate of this population (eleven suicides for every hundred thousand people) is higher than for any other age group, and the attempts are serious: One out of four succeeds, compared with one out of two hundred for young adults.

Depression in Children and Teens

Until recently, many doctors and other professionals did not believe that children could be depressed. Recent research shows that children can suffer from many of the same depressive disorders as adults. Although the onset of depression is typically between the ages of twenty and forty, recent research shows that the average age of onset is decreasing with each generation. Today, about 2.5 million people under the age of eighteen in the United States are diagnosed with major depression. As teenagers get older, their risk of experiencing depression increases. According to the U.S. Department of Health and Human Services, 5.4 percent of twelve- to thirteen-year-olds are depressed, but 12.3 percent of sixteen- to seventeen-year-olds suffer from depression.

Unfortunately, depression in young people often goes undiagnosed. Parents often assume that signs of illness are "just a phase." As a result, fewer than half of children and teens with depression receive treatment. Left untreated, childhood depression often continues into adulthood. Many people who have minor depression as children will experience more severe illnesses in adulthood.

As children, boys and girls are equally likely to develop depressive disorders. By age fifteen, however, girls are twice as likely as boys to have had a major depressive episode. Some experts believe the higher rate among adolescent girls may be due to both biology and environmental factors. Changes in the levels of female hormones during puberty may be to blame. In addition, the fact that girls are more socially oriented than boys may make girls more vulnerable to feelings of loss and despair following a breakup with a close friend.

Adolescence brings on a great many physical and emotional changes. Breaking away from one's parents, making decisions on one's own, grappling with issues related to dating, dealing with peer pressure, deciding where to go to college or what to do with one's future—these are just a few of the stresses faced by today's teens. Many experts believe these new stresses contribute to the risk of clinical depression for both boys and girls.

According to the Center for Mental Health Services, about one in every ten teens in the United States suffers from some type of depression. Depression among teens frequently coincides with anxiety, eating disorders, or substance abuse. It also increases the risk of teen suicide.

Health Risks

Depression can have a major impact on sufferers' health. People with depression are at greater risk of developing other physical illnesses. Experts caution that those suffering from depression may be less likely to go to the doctor when they are sick and/or to heed the doctor's advice. Research also suggests that depression and the resulting stress weakens the immune system and reduces its ability to fight infection. Studies show that vaccinations are less effective in people with depression, leaving them more vulnerable to illness.

Recent studies have also shown that people with depression who are recovering from strokes or heart attacks have more difficulty making health care choices, following a doctor's instructions, and coping with the challenges that such illnesses present. Studies also have linked depression to heart disease. One study found that patients with depression also have a higher risk of death in the first few months after a heart attack.

The more severe the symptoms of depression, the greater the impact on a person's day-to-day life. People suffering from a mild form of the illness might be able to continue their usual activities, although they might not find them quite as enjoyable. As depression takes hold, however, it might take more and more effort to get up in the morning, leave the house, and concentrate at school or work. In severe cases of depression, any activity beyond simply surviving can become difficult.

People with especially severe symptoms may turn to alcohol or drugs to cope with their depression.

Another health risk associated with depression is alcohol and drug abuse, particularly among teens and young males. When the pain of depression becomes overwhelming, too many people attempt to drown it through drugs or alcohol. Experts call this destructive behavior "self-medicating." A 2004 study by the U.S. Department of Health and Human Services reports that teens with depression were almost twice as likely to use alcohol, illegal drugs, and cigarettes as those who did not have depression.

Drugs and alcohol may seem like a way to cope with depressive symptoms, but they lead to deeper problems. Alcohol itself is a depressant. It does not alleviate depressive symptoms; in fact, it has the opposite effect. Some people who turn to drugs become addicted, trading one set of problems for another. Becoming dependent on drugs and alcohol can further erode one's sense of self-worth and add to physical health problems.

Suicide is another problem associated with depression. Most people who suffer from depression do not attempt suicide, but this is a very real risk, particularly for those who do not seek treatment. According to the National Mental Health Association, 41 percent of people with depression have contemplated suicide. An estimated 30 to 70 percent of suicide victims have suffered from some form of depression.

Impact on Society

Depression affects not only the person who is suffering from the disorder but also family and friends. At home, depressed people sometimes lack interest in or concern for their family and friends. They are often unable to demonstrate affection for loved ones. They may avoid friends and social gatherings.

Living with a depressed person can be very difficult. Depression often strains relationships with family members. Friendships may crumble. As family members and friends become more distant, the depressed person may feel abandoned and even more worthless, exacerbating the depression.

Depression also takes a toll on society at large. At work, people with depression tend to be slower and less productive than healthier individuals. They also tend to be indecisive and uncertain. The inability to concentrate may result in more mistakes. Depression can also cause people to miss work. People suffering from major depression sometimes find it hard to get out of bed in the morning and may be likely to take more sick leave. Depression can also cause headaches, stomachaches, or chronic pain, which may result in missed work. A recent study undertaken by the Rand Corporation found that patients with depressive symptoms spend more days in bed than those with diabetes, arthritis, back problems, lung problems, or gastrointestinal disorders.

Experts have also studied the impact on workers. Research from the National Institute of Mental Health (NIMH) concludes that each worker in the United States with major depression lost an average of 27.2 workdays per year. Another study, published in the *Journal of the American Medical Association*, found that 9.4 percent of workers struggle with depression and that, on average, these employees lose 5.6 productive hours per week in work absences and reduced performance time due to their depression. NIMH also reports that most of the lost time—81 percent—occurs while employees are at work. Together, the missed work and the decreased productivity cost U.S. businesses about $44 billion a year.

While $44 billion a year is a staggering figure—more than the cost of almost any other disease—this figure accounts for only the depressed individuals. It does not include the costs of work lost by their family members, friends, or coworkers. For example, the caregiver of a spouse or child with depression might have to take time from work to care for their loved one. Studies suggest that caregivers, too, suffer from lower concentration, morale, and productivity. Some experts say the total economic effect of depression is incalculable because these estimates also fail to account for the inefficiencies of depressed and distracted employees who remain at work.

The medical costs of depression for the afflicted also go beyond medication and therapy. Many depressed people have unexplained pain or illnesses. They go to the doctor seeking relief from the symptoms, but the problem remains untreated. As the issue is unresolved, the visits to the doctor—and expenses—continue to add up. In addition, depressed people often stop

Depression takes a huge financial toll on society in terms of lost productivity in the workplace and the medical costs of treatment.

caring for themselves. This can lead to many medical problems and their attendant expenses, particularly if the depression is left untreated for a prolonged period of time.

Fortunately, depression can be alleviated with treatment. Mental health advocates urge businesses to have employee assistance programs where employees can get help for their problems and health insurance that will reduce financial obstacles. Still, many people suffering from depression fail to get help. In some cases people are ashamed to admit they have a problem. Others might fail to recognize the symptoms of depression. Mary Ellen Copeland, an author, educator, and mental health advocate who has suffered from major depression and bipolar disorder, says that she learned to recognize warning signs of a depressive episode:

> There is a hard, dark, very murky lump that aches a bit in the middle of my chest. It is gray, but not the warm gray of tree trunks or chick-a-dees. It is a foreboding and sinister gray, one that has the capacity to sap my life energy and spiral me down into the pits of despair. This is a warning— a warning that if I don't notice it, and slowly excise it, it will grow until it encompasses all of my being, sending me for weeks, maybe months into the depths of discouragement and despair—a condition that has no redeeming features and leaves me feeling empty and alone. Through years of recurring severe depressions, I have come to know what that lump means. I know I have to hurry to get rid of it, before it claims any more of my being—before the energy it takes to erase it is gone.[13]

The sense of hopelessness that is symptomatic of depression can be an obstacle for the very people most in need of treatment. Some people with depression may lack the energy needed to make a phone call or keep an appointment with a doctor or therapist. The first step is to recognize the warning signs and understand the many factors that can contribute to depression.

CHAPTER TWO

Causes of Depression

Over the years, people have argued about what causes depression. Some experts argue that a person's genetic makeup determines whether he or she is susceptible, or genetically predisposed, to depression. They point to the fact that depression runs in families. Others downplay the role of genetics, arguing that depression is caused by stress, trauma, or physical or mental illness.

Today, most experts believe depression results from a combination of genetic, biochemical, environmental, and psychological factors. In some cases depression may spring from purely biological factors. Heredity appears to play an important role: People with relatives who have had depression are more likely to suffer from the disease themselves. In addition, having a family history of alcoholism, bipolar disorder, schizophrenia, or other mental illness also increases the risk of depression. However, depression can occur in people without a family history of mental illness. In some cases trauma, the death of a loved one, a difficult relationship, or other stressful situations may trigger a depressive episode; in other cases, an episode may occur without an obvious trigger.

Depression and the Brain

Like a complex computer, the human brain serves as the "command center" of the human body. The brain controls basic automatic, unconscious functions, such as the heart's pumping of blood through the body. A small structure at the base

The Impact of Lifestyle

Where and how a person lives may influence the risk of depression. Not surprisingly, people living in northern regions where there is less sunlight are more likely to experience seasonal affective disorder. In addition, some evidence suggests that people living in urban areas may be at greater risk than those in rural communities. In fact, one study found that major depression is twice as common among people who live in cities than those who live in rural areas.

Having a network of close family and friends reduces the risk of depression. The rate of depression is higher among people who live alone than among those who live with family or room-mates. Depression is higher among divorced and separated adults than among married people and singles. Also, higher rates than average are found among the homosexual population.

Research comparing the rates of depression among different races and ethnic groups has been inconclusive. Some studies in the United States suggest that the rate of depression is higher among whites than African Americans and Hispanics, but other studies have refuted these findings. Regardless of race or ethnicity, a higher rate of depression is found where poverty exists; rates are especially high among the homeless population. Research also shows that the rate of depression among people who have been unemployed for six months or more in the last five years is three times that of the general population.

of the brain, the hypothalamus, automatically regulates body temperature, sleep, and appetite. The brain also controls emotions and mood.

Neurons and neurotransmitters play an important role in the processes of the body. Neurons are nerve cells in the brain that are organized to control specialized activities. In the brain, 100 billion neurons transmit messages from one to another in the form of chemicals, called neurotransmitters, which carry the messages through the synapses—the narrow gaps that separate the neurons. These chemical messengers travel across the neurons at an amazing rate of speed—less than 1/5,000 of a second—allowing people to react instantaneously and unconsciously to pain or other stimuli.

Neurotransmitters travel from neuron to neuron in an orderly fashion. They are specifically shaped so that after they pass from a neuron into the synapse, they can be received onto certain sites, called receptors, on another neuron. Upon landing at the receptor site, the neurotransmitter may either be changed into an electrical impulse and continue on its way through the next neuron, or it may stop where it is. In either case the neurotransmitter leaves the receptor site and floats back into the synapse. There, it can either be broken down by a chemical, or it can be reabsorbed by the neuron that initially released it, a process called reuptake.

Research has shown that some forms of mental illness occur when too many or too few neurotransmitters are present or when a problem interferes with the way the neurotransmitters are released or broken down. Unfortunately, neurotransmitters are difficult to study because they exist only in very small quantities and disappear very quickly once they are used, but research has begun to yield some information about how neurotransmitters might influence emotions and behavior. Of the roughly thirty neurotransmitters that scientists have identified, three may play a particular role in depression: serotonin, norepinephrine, and dopamine. These three neurotransmitters function within structures of the brain that regulate emotions, reactions to stress, and the physical drives of sleep, appetite, and sex.

Serotonin was among the first neurotransmitters to be identified and linked to depression. High levels of serotonin are associated with aggression and poor sleep quality. Low levels are associated with irritability, anxiety, lethargy, and suicidal thoughts and behaviors. Brain imaging studies confirm that the serotonin transporter involved in regulating the serotonin varies by season, leading scientists to speculate that imbalances

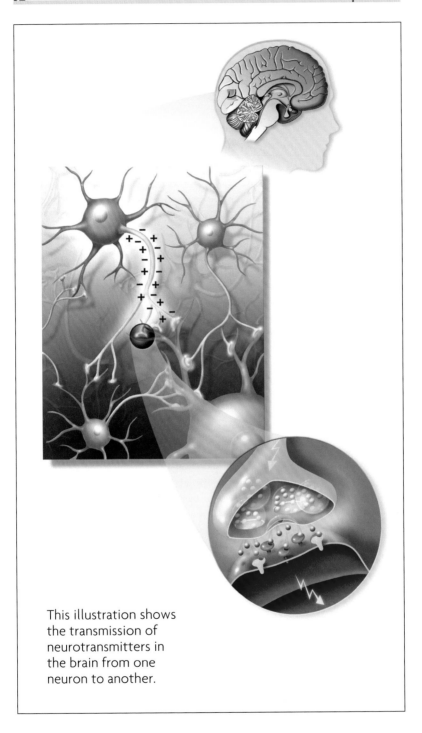

This illustration shows
the transmission of
neurotransmitters in
the brain from one
neuron to another.

of serotonin caused by too much or too little sunlight may be responsible for seasonal affective disorder. Many of the popular antidepressant medications on the market today act to increase the amount of serotonin in the brain.

Dopamine has also been linked to depression. Dopamine influences emotion, motor movements, learning, thinking, memory, and attention. Too little dopamine can induce depression.

The link between these neurotransmitters and depression is not always clear, however. Research has shown that many people who are depressed have low levels of norepinephrine, for instance, which regulates the "fight-or-flight" response to perceived danger in the environment. While scientists have associated a low level of this neurotransmitter with depression, some people with clinical depression have unusually high levels. Experts caution that this also may be true for other neurotransmitters. Researchers disagree about the cause-and-effect relationship between neurotransmitters and depression. They are not sure whether a low level of one of these chemicals causes depression or whether it is the depression that lowers the amount of the chemical.

Scientists also believe that other abnormalities in the brain may cause depression. Studies using brain-imaging technologies, such as magnetic resonance imaging (MRI), have shown that the brains of people who have depression look different than those of people without depression. For instance, the hippocampus—a specialized area of the brain involved in memory and emotion—is smaller in people with chronic depression.

Hormones and the Endocrine System

Research has shown that many people who are depressed have abnormal levels of some hormones. Changes in hormones are thought to play a major role in postpartum depression, for instance. It is believed that abnormal levels of some hormones—or rapid fluctuations in these levels—may result in depressive symptoms such as problems with appetite and sleeping.

About half of those individuals who are clinically depressed have an excess of the hormone cortisol in their blood. Cortisol is secreted by the adrenal glands. Located on the kidneys, the adrenal glands influence reactions to stressful events. Scientists believe that cortisol may be related to depression because as symptoms of depression disappear, the levels of this hormone usually return to normal. Scientists also believe that abnormal levels of hormones, such as testosterone in men and progester-

This illustration of glands in the endocrine system shows the pituitary gland (enlarged, inset), which produces a hormone that stimulates the adrenal glands (atop the kidneys, bottom) to produce the hormone cortisol.

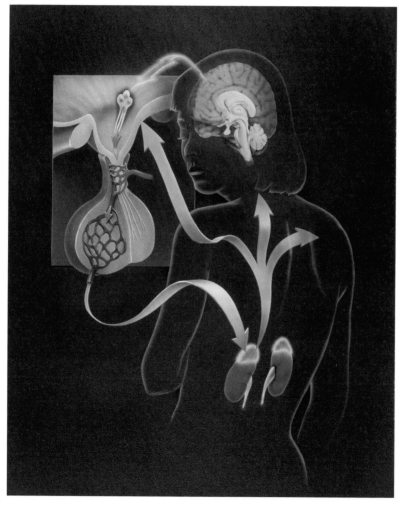

one and estrogen in women, may be the culprits in the onset of some types of depression.

The relationship between hormones and depression has led scientists to believe the endocrine system may play an important role in the disease. The endocrine system is the system of small glands that create hormones and release them into the bloodstream. The endocrine system is connected with the brain at the hypothalamus. A healthy endocrine system keeps hormone levels at a relatively constant state through an intricate process of feedback, much like a thermostat in a home. When the endocrine system is not functioning properly, the brain may fail to receive the message that sufficient amounts of hormones are already in the bloodstream. The adrenal glands—which are part of the endocrine system—may continue to secrete hormones without regard to the amount that is already in the blood. Scientists believe this malfunction results in many of the symptoms characteristic of depression.

Depression also may be a symptom of a disorder or disease in the organs that produce hormones. Conditions such as thyroid disorders, Cushing's syndrome, and Addison's disease can increase a person's risk of depression.

The Role of Genes

A person with a parent or sibling who has had major depression is 1.5 to 3 times more likely to develop the condition than people who do not. Because depression tends to run in families, scientists have deduced that genes may play an important role. Genes are the part of deoxyribonucleic acid (DNA) that carry information from parent to child. Genes are responsible for physical attributes such as eye color, hair color, and height. Scientists believe that genes may also carry information about one's susceptibility to diseases such as depression. According to the NIMH, "Researchers are increasingly certain that genes play an important role in vulnerability to depression and other severe mental disorders."[14]

Still, genetic research is inconclusive. So far, no research has shown a specific gene or genes to be responsible for the disorder. Most scientists today believe that the risk for depression results from the influence of multiple genes acting together with environmental or other factors.

Other Risk Factors

In addition to genetic and other biological causes of depression, a wide range of environmental factors can trigger a depressive episode. The death of a loved one, a financial crisis, loss of a job, and divorce are common triggers. A major depressive episode can also be prompted by a seemingly happy life change, such as a new baby, new job, or graduation from school. Even the weather is thought to contribute to the risk of depression, as evidenced by the hundreds of thousands of people who suffer from seasonal affective disorder. Subsequent depressive episodes may occur with or without an obvious trigger.

Researchers also suggest that stress experienced during childhood may also play a role. Physical, sexual, or psychological abuse, neglect, the early loss of a parent, or living with a parent who abuses alcohol or drugs can increase the risk of depression many years later. Children living in families troubled with divorce or ongoing marital, financial, or other problems may also suffer from depression as adults. Scientists believe that this may be due to the stress brought on by these situations.

Depression and Illness

Depression often coexists with other illnesses. Such illnesses may cause the depression and/or be a consequence of the disease. Even in cases in which depression and another illness may not have a causal relationship, appropriate treatment of depression depends on recognizing the role of coexisting illnesses.

Heart disease, cancer, HIV/AIDS, diabetes, and Parkinson's disease are among the many serious medical conditions associated with depression. Studies have shown that people with heart disease are more depressed than healthy people, for instance. While about one in six people experiences an episode of major depression, the number goes to one in two for people with heart disease.

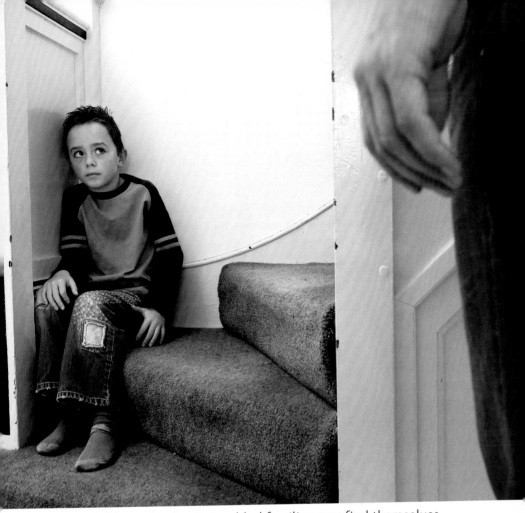

Children who live in troubled families may find themselves suffering from depression when they become adults.

Chronic illness may lead to depression or increase its severity, in part because of the weakness and stress that accompany a serious medical condition. Just getting through the day can be difficult for people who are in constant pain or have a disability that prevents them from doing what they want to do.

Studies have shown that people who have depression in addition to another serious medical condition tend to have more severe symptoms, greater difficulty adapting to their medical condition, and higher medical costs than patients who do not suffer from depression. Among these patients, increasing evidence suggests that treating the depression can help

"Depression Can Break Your Heart"

Some research on depression has focused on the relationship between depression and other life-threatening illnesses. The National Institute of Mental Health has sponsored a number of studies. In an article titled "Depression Can Break Your Heart," the NIMH writes of the relationship between depression and heart disease:

> Research over the past two decades has shown that depression and heart disease are common companions and what is worse, each can lead to the other. It appears now that depression is an important risk factor for heart disease along with high blood cholesterol and high blood pressure.
>
> Depression may make it harder to take the medications needed and to carry out the treatment for heart disease. Depression may also result in chronically elevated levels of stress hormones, such as cortisol and adrenaline, and the activation of the sympathetic nervous system (part of the "fight or flight" response), which can have deleterious effects on the heart.

Stress, Anxiety & Depression Resource Center, "Depression Can Break Your Heart," June 3, 2009. www.stress-anxiety-depression.org/depression/can-break-heart.html.

improve patient outcomes, regardless of the extent and type of the coexisting illness. Doctors also caution that depression is sometimes an unanticipated side effect of the drugs used to treat medical conditions.

Anxiety and Depression

Anxiety disorders often accompany depression. Anxiety takes many different forms. Some people with anxiety disorders suffer panic attacks, which are sudden bouts of fear accompanied by a racing heart and breathlessness. In other forms of anxiety, people relive traumatic events from their past. People suffering from anxiety may be terrified of crowds or specific events or of objects such as elevators or bridges.

One form of anxiety that is particularly common with depression is post-traumatic stress disorder (PTSD). PTSD is a debilitating condition that results from a terrifying event or ordeal, such as a violent assault, natural disaster, or military

Some people with depression also suffer from an anxiety disorder. In such cases a patient must be treated for both conditions.

combat. In an NIMH study, researchers found that more than 40 percent of people with PTSD also suffered from depression following the traumatic event that triggered the PTSD.

Like depression, anxiety is treatable with therapy, medication, or a combination of both. The effectiveness of treatment for depression when it is accompanied by an anxiety disorder depends on treating the patient both for depression and anxiety.

Alcohol and Drug Abuse

Alcohol and other substance abuse also sometimes coexist with depression. A number of studies have shown that alcohol abuse or dependence is associated with major depression. An estimated 30 percent to 50 percent of people with alcoholism also suffer from major depression. Suicide rates are higher among people with coexisting alcoholism and depression.

Research has been inconclusive about whether one of those disorders causes the other, or whether a common underlying genetic or environmental risk factor increases the risk for both. Experts have long believed that people suffering from depression may "self-medicate" with alcohol or drugs to alleviate the symptoms. Other research—including a twenty-five-year study by scientists in New Zealand—concludes that alcohol abuse or dependence increases the risk of developing clinical depression. "The best-fitting model was one in which there was a unidirectional association from alcohol abuse or dependence to major depression but no reverse effect from major depression to alcohol abuse or dependence," the authors report. "In addition, further research suggests that alcohol's depressant characteristics may lead to periods of depressed affect among those with alcohol abuse or dependence."[15]

Similarly, depression is sometimes associated with the use of illegal recreational drugs, such as marijuana, ecstasy, and heroin. As with alcohol, a person who is suffering from depressive symptoms may take drugs in the hope of gaining some relief, or depressive symptoms may develop as a direct result of taking drugs. In some cases, depression is a symptom of withdrawal when a person stops taking a drug.

Persons with depression may also abuse alcohol, a deadly combination, since the incidence of suicide is higher in such individuals.

Also important to note is that some prescription drugs have also been linked to depressive symptoms. Sedatives such as Valium (diazepam) and pain medications such as Percocet (oxycodone and acetaminophen) and Demerol (meperidine) have been linked to depression. Psychiatrists warn that some depressed people may take a high dose of these or other pre-scription drugs in an attempt to end their life.

Causes and Treatment

Our understanding of the direct causes of depression and the factors that influence the risk of a depressive episode is chang-ing. People once believed that depression—like other mental illnesses—was the result of an imbalance of bodily fluids or a sign of being possessed by demons. Today, doctors have linked the disorder to brain chemistry. Still, scientists admit there is much they do not know. A better understanding of the causes of depression could help with prevention, early diagnosis, and treatment.

CHAPTER THREE

Treatment for Depression

Depression, even in the most severe cases, is a highly treatable disorder. As with many illnesses, the earlier that treatment can begin, the more effective it is and the greater the likelihood that recurrence can be prevented. Once identified, most people diagnosed with depression are successfully treated. Unfortunately depression is not always diagnosed because many of the symptoms mimic physical illness, such as sleep and appetite disturbances. Recognizing depression is the first step in treating it. Properly diagnosed, even the most severe cases of depression can be treated, enabling those suffering from the illness to lead productive and happy lives.

Actor and comedian Jim Carrey has suffered from depressive episodes all his life. "I was on Prozac for a long time," he said in an interview with *60 Minutes*. "It may have helped me out of a jam for a little bit, but people stay on it forever. I had to get off at a certain point because I realized that, you know, everything's just OK."[16]

Carrey stopped taking antidepressants for a more holistic, spiritual approach to combating his demons. "I rarely drink coffee," he says. "I'm very serious about no alcohol, no drugs. Life is too beautiful. . . . I'm a Buddhist, I'm a Muslim, I'm a Christian. I'm whatever you want me to be. It all comes down to the same thing: You are either in a loving place, or you are in an unloving place."[17]

Getting Help

Experts believe that more than half of all people suffering from depression do not get proper treatment. In many cases the people who are suffering from depression and their loved ones may not recognize the symptoms. A person may assume that his or her spouse is lazy; a teacher or supervisor at work might think poor concentration is a sign of disinterest; a parent might assume that a child who is acting out is going through a difficult phase. Thus, it can take years for the symptoms to be recognized as worthy of professional attention.

Misdiagnosis on the part of doctors is another problem. Sometimes medical professionals misdiagnose depression and treat the symptoms without recognizing that they are a sign of depression. People with depression may be given treatment for stomach problems or migraines without anyone realizing that depression is the root of these ailments.

Some people—especially men—may not seek out treatment because they believe that doing so is a sign of weakness. As the depression goes untreated, it may deepen. People with serious depression may lack the energy or will to reach out for help. "It felt as though the world was spinning too fast," says Linda, a twenty-nine-year-old single woman who was dealing with an ailing mother and a divorce. "I knew there was something wrong, but I barely had enough energy to get out of bed. I just didn't want to deal with anything."[18]

The first step in the treatment of depression, as with any illness, is to recognize the symptoms and seek help from a medical professional. A proper diagnosis is essential for determining the correct treatment, as different types of depression are treated with different medications.

Diagnosis

Often, the first step in diagnosing depression involves ruling out other illnesses that may have the same symptoms. A physical examination can help a doctor figure out whether the symptoms are caused by a virus or perhaps an enlarged thyroid; lab tests are usually used to measure the level of hormones in the

If an individual suspects he or she may be depressed, seeing a doctor for a thorough analysis of the symptoms is critical. If untreated, depression worsens.

blood and urine as part of this process. Typically prescription drugs, vitamin supplements, and other medications the patient is taking are reviewed to make sure that the symptoms are not a side effect of a drug or caused by a drug interaction.

Once the doctor has ruled out other possible causes, the patient typically undergoes psychological diagnostic testing. Diagnostic testing is sometimes done by a general practitioner or a mental health professional such as a psychologist or psychiatrist. Careful analysis of the symptoms, including their onset and severity, can help determine whether depression is the cause. The professional also typically explores the many factors that may put a person at risk for depression, including family history, stress and trauma, medical conditions, alcohol and drug use, suicidal thoughts or inclinations, and past experience with depressive-type mood disorders.

A thorough diagnostic evaluation also includes a mental health examination to assess the full range of psychological symptoms. This information is used to evaluate the type of depression the person has—whether it is major depression, dysthymia, bipolar disorder, or some other depressive disorder. The mental health diagnostic information can also be used to help identify any other psychological problems that might be present. The more information that is gathered during the diagnostic process, the better the professional will be able to tailor treatment to the specific needs of the patient.

Diagnostic testing is used to identify and characterize symptoms. In general the diagnostic criteria for mental disorders fall into one of four categories: affective, behavioral, cognitive, and somatic. In clinical depression, affective, or mood, symptoms may include depressed mood and feelings of worthlessness, hopelessness, or guilt. Behavioral symptoms include social withdrawal and agitation. Cognitive symptoms, or those involving thinking, include poor concentration or indecisiveness. Finally, somatic, or physical, symptoms include changes in sleep or appetite.

Treatment Options

Once diagnosed, depression can be treated in a number of ways. Usually, the medical doctor and/or mental health professional will work with the patient to draw up an appropriate treatment plan. An estimated 80 percent of people with major depression can make significant progress, but success depends on finding the right therapies. Depression can be particularly difficult to treat in children, adolescents, elderly patients, and those with a history of chronic disease.

Treatment options vary considerably. Factors influencing decisions about appropriate treatment include the type and severity of the depression and its symptoms. If the patient has received treatment in the past, the plan will build on what worked; effective therapies used for members of the patient's family might also be included in the treatment plan.

The most common treatments are medication and one of many different types of psychotherapy, including sessions that try to uncover some of the underlying reasons for a depressive episode, and cognitive-behavioral therapy, which focuses on

Common Antidepressant Drugs

Many of the newest drug classes have only one drug, but as scientists and pharmaceutical companies continue to look for the perfect antidote to depression, additional medications will likely join these options in the coming years. The classes of anti-depressants on the market today include:

Drug Class	Chemical/ Generic Name	Brand Name
Tricyclic antibiodies (TCAs)	imipramine amitriptyline clomipramine nortriptyline desipramine	Tofranil Elavil Anafranil Pamelor Norpramin
Monoamine oxidase inhibitors (MAOIs)	phenelzine tranylcypromine	Nardil Parnate
Reversible inhibitors of monoamine oxidase (RIMAs)	moclobemide	Manerix
Selective serotonin reuptake inhibitors (SSRIs)	fluoxetine fluvoxemine paroxetine sertraline citalopram	Prozac Luvox Paxil Zoloft Celexa
Serotonin and norepinephrine reuptake inhibitors (SNRIs)	venlafaxine duloxetine	Effexor Cymbalta
Norepinephrine and dopamine reuptake inhibitors (NDRIs)	bupropion	Wellbutrin
Serotonin-2 antagonist/ reuptake inhibitors (SARIs)	nefazodone	Serzone
Serotonin 2, 3 antagonist and serotonin-norepinephrine reuptake inhibitor (SA/SNRIs)	mirtazapine	Remeron

teaching people how to change their thoughts and behaviors. Experts disagree about whether either of these treatments can be effective on its own. Some doctors prescribe antidepressant drugs without referring patients to psychotherapy, but some professionals warn that drugs do not "cure" the depression; they treat only its symptoms. For this reason experts caution that psychotherapy—or "talk" therapy, in which a patient meets regularly with a mental health professional—is a critical element of treatment. Advocates of psychotherapy believe that it can help people understand the factors that trigger a depressive episode and can help them learn more effective ways of dealing with stress and other problems.

Drug Treatment

Prescription antidepressant medications are often the first treatment option for adults with recurring and persistent forms of depression. According to the Centers for Disease Control and Prevention (CDC), antidepressants are the most commonly prescribed medication in the country. The *International Review of Psychiatry* reported in June 2005 that more than 67.5 million Americans—almost one in four people—have taken a course of antidepressant medication during their lifetimes.

Antidepressants work to normalize the neurotransmitters in the brain that impact mood, notably serotonin, norepinephrine, and dopamine. The most popular types of antidepressant medications are called selective serotonin reuptake inhibitors (SSRIs). SSRIs increase the level of serotonin by stopping the sending neuron from reabsorbing it. The most widely prescribed SSRIs on the market today include fluoxetine (Prozac), paroxetine (Paxil), and sertraline (Zoloft). Serotonin and norepinephrine reuptake inhibitors (SNRIs) are similar to SSRIs, but they stop the reuptake of norepinephrine as well as serotonin. SNRIs include venlafaxine (Effexor) and duloxetine (Cymbalta). While SSRIs and SNRIs are considered the newest class of antidepressant drugs, some of these drugs have been on the market for more than twenty years. SSRIs have quickly become popular because they are effective for a wide variety of symptoms and tend to have fewer side effects than older classes of antidepressants.

Some patients respond better to other classes of antidepressant drugs, such as monoamine oxidase inhibitors (MAOIs) or tricyclics. MAOIs work by irreversibly changing the enzyme (monoamine oxidase) that breaks down neurotransmitters, so that norepinephrine and serotonin increase in the synapses. MAOIs have proved particularly effective in depression that manifests itself with increased appetite and need for sleep. Tricyclic antibodies, which block the reuptake of norepinephrine into the sending neuron, work well among adult men, in severe cases with many physical symptoms, and in cases marked by excessive fatigue and lethargy. They are less often used in young or elderly patients because they increase heart rate and lower blood pressure.

Antidepressants do not work the same for every patient, and which drug or combination of drugs will work best in each case is not always clear. NIMH-funded research has shown that patients whose symptoms were not improved by one medication often became symptom free when switching to a different drug. Fortunately for patients and doctors, with continued pharmaceutical research the options continue to expand.

A doctor must sometimes prescribe several different medications before determining which drug works best for a particular patient.

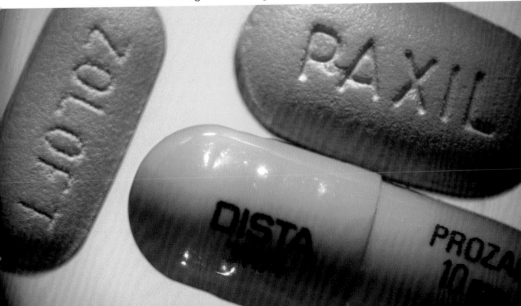

In addition to an antidepressant, some patients with depression are prescribed a stimulant, anti-anxiety medication, or other medication. This can be particularly important for patients who have coexisting mental or physical conditions.

Rarely do antidepressants work immediately. Many patients take the drugs for three to four weeks before they experience a full therapeutic effect. Patients may have to try different levels of a medication to find the right dosage. It may be tempting for patients to stop taking the antidepressant as their symptoms subside, but doctors warn that symptoms may recur if patients do not take an antidepressant as prescribed.

The risk of addiction to an antidepressant is almost nonexistent, but patients who abruptly stop taking an antidepressant can experience unpleasant withdrawal symptoms. As a result, patients are usually weaned off antidepressants gradually. Usually, a doctor works closely with patients to make sure that ceasing a medication does not result in a return of symptoms.

Some people—including those who have chronic depression or recurring major depressive episodes—may need to take antidepressants for life. Terry Bradshaw, an NFL quarterback with the Pittsburgh Steelers, could not seem to bounce back from a divorce. He experienced frequent anxiety, crying jags, weight loss, and sleeplessness—all symptoms of major depression that were treated with antidepressants. "When you're clinically depressed the serotonin in your brain is out of balance and probably always will be out of balance. So I take medication to get that proper balance back. I'll probably have to be on it the rest of my life." Bradshaw says the drugs have been effective, however. "The beauty of it is that there are medications that work. Look at me. I'm always happy-go-lucky, and people look at me and find it shocking that I could be depressed."[19]

Side Effects and Adverse Reactions

All medications have potential side effects, and antidepressants are no exception. Side effects sometimes associated with SSRIs include headaches, gastrointestinal problems, and

Antidepressants and Suicide

On October 15, 2004, in response to clinical trials that showed evidence of a connection between the use of antidepressants in children and an increased risk of suicide and suicidal thinking, the U.S. Food and Drug Administration (FDA) ordered drug manufacturers to add a "black box" warning to the label of antidepressants. The black box is the most serious type of warning issued by the FDA. An excerpt from the warning reads:

> Antidepressants increase the risk of suicidal thinking and behavior (suicidality) in children and adolescents with major depressive disorder (MDD) and other psychiatric disorders. Anyone considering the use of [Drug Name] or any other antidepressant in a child or adolescent must balance this risk with the clinical need. Patients who are started on therapy should be observed closely for clinical worsening, suicidality, or unusual changes in behavior. Families and caregivers should be advised of the need for close observation and communication with the prescriber.

In May 2007 the FDA recommended that the warning be expanded to include young adults from ages eighteen to twenty-four. Certain young adults are at an even greater risk for suicide when taking antidepressants, including those with bipolar disorder, a family history of bipolar disorder, or a history of previous suicide attempts. The risk of suicide is particularly great during the first one to two months of antidepressant treatment. FDA guidelines instruct young adults to see their doctor weekly during the first four weeks of starting on an antidepressant or changing the dosage.

nausea, but these are usually temporary. SSRIs can also cause insomnia or early morning waking, particularly during the first few weeks the drug is taken. Agitation and sexual problems may be longer-lasting side effects of this class of drugs.

Some studies have suggested that SSRIs may have serious negative side effects on some people, especially adolescents and young adults. In a 2004 Food and Drug Administration (FDA) review of clinical trials undertaken, 4 percent of people taking antidepressants thought about or attempted suicide, compared with 2 percent of people who were receiving placebos. This information prompted the FDA to alert the public by requiring all antidepressant medications to display a "black box" label warning about the potential increased risk of suicidal thinking or attempts in children and adolescents taking antidepressants. A black box warning is the most serious type of warning on prescription drug labeling.

In adults over the age of sixty-five, some antidepressants pose an additional concern. Studies show that SSRI medications may increase the risk for falls, fractures, and bone loss in older adults. SSRIs can also cause serious withdrawal symptoms if patients abruptly stop taking them.

Tricyclic antidepressants (TCAs) have some of the same side effects as SSRIs, including gastrointestinal and sexual problems. People taking TCAs also sometimes experience blurred vision, fainting, and drowsiness, leading doctors often to recommend that they be taken at bedtime. An overdose can be fatal.

MAOIs tend to have a higher risk of toxicity than SSRIs or SNRIs. Dangerous interactions can occur when MAOIs are taken with foods that have high levels of a chemical called tyramine, which is found in many cheeses, smoked meats and fish, beer and wines, avocados, tofu, dried figs, and several other foods. Eating these foods while taking MAOIs can cause a sharp increase in blood pressure, which can lead to a stroke. MAOIs also can have dangerous interactions with several over-the-counter medications, including decongestants, cough medicines, and weight-loss pills.

Limitations of Drug Therapy

While studies—and stories from individual patients—seem to bolster many of the claims of manufacturers and supporters of antidepressant medications, critics say that their supposed benefits may be due to the "placebo effect," which means that the patient feels better simply because he or she thinks that treatment has been provided and not as a result of the medication itself.

Some medical professionals believe that antidepressants are prescribed too often to people suffering "normal" symptoms related to stress or life's difficulties. Experts also caution that antidepressants may not be effective in treating many mild forms of depression. A 2002 study of adults who had received a prescription for an antidepressant found that just 20 percent tested positive when screened for depression, and fewer than 30 percent had any depressive symptoms at all. One critic of prescription antidepressants writes, "Antidepressants are replacing tranquilizers as the mood-altering drug of choice, based on the questionable notion that anxious, restless, agitated, irritable, and diagnosis-starved patients are actually suffering from depression."[20]

Still, many medical professionals believe it is far better to risk prescribing an antidepressant to a patient who may not need it than to risk withholding medication from someone with depression. Not only do antidepressants help depressed people function, they may lessen the risk of suicide. In cases of severe depression, antidepressants may save lives by eliminating the desire to commit suicide. A fifteen-year study in Sweden showed that increased antidepressant prescribing was associated with a decrease in suicide rates.

Psychotherapy

Psychotherapy, or "talk therapy," can play a critical role in treating many forms of depression. Mental health experts emphasize that psychotherapy is particularly important in treatment plans for children and teens. Pyschotherapy is generally provided by a psychiatrist or licensed psychologist, social worker, or counselor. Some patients may see gains in a relatively short period of time, meeting weekly for ten or twenty weeks perhaps, while for other patients the therapy may continue indefinitely. As with other aspects of the treatment plan, this depends on the patient, the type of depression, and the severity of the symptoms.

The approaches of psychotherapy used to treat depression are many and varied. Generally, they fall into two categories, cognitive-behavioral therapy and interpersonal therapy. Cognitive-behavioral therapy focuses on new ways of thinking to change behavior; the therapist helps patients change negative or unproductive patterns that may contribute to their depression. Interpersonal therapy helps people understand and work through difficult situations and relationships that may be causing or contributing to their depression.

Many people find that psychotherapy is sufficient to helping them overcome their depression, particularly when the symptoms are mild. When a depressive episode is triggered by an external event, for instance, meeting with a mental health professional can help people sort out their feelings and learn how to cope.

Research suggests that patients who rely only on psychotherapy as treatment for major depression may have a greater risk of recurring illness. Still, although experts caution that psychotherapy alone may not work for people with ongoing major depression, some people with lifelong symptoms find that they can wean themselves off antidepressants if they continue psychotherapy treatment.

While meeting one-on-one with a therapist is often highly beneficial, some treatment plans involve the entire family. The therapist may meet with the family to help reduce the stress that may result from having a member with depression, as well as resolve the issues that may be contributing factors to the depression. The therapist can also offer resources to help family members better understand and accept depression as a mental illness, not something that the patient is likely to simply "snap out of." Family therapy may also focus on improving communication and problem-solving skills among family members. Studies suggest that family therapy may be an important component of effective treatment.

While medications can be quite effective for depression sufferers, psychotherapy, or "talk therapy," can also play an important role in treatment.

Electroconvulsive Therapy

In the mid–twentieth century electroconvulsive therapy (ECT)—known then as "shock therapy"—was the main treatment option for severe depression. ECT works by passing electric currents through the brain, deliberately causing a brief seizure. The procedure seems to change brain chemistry, resulting in improved mood, perhaps because it releases so many neurotransmitters simultaneously and speeds up functioning. ECT earned a negative reputation stemming from the early days of its use, when it was administered at high doses without

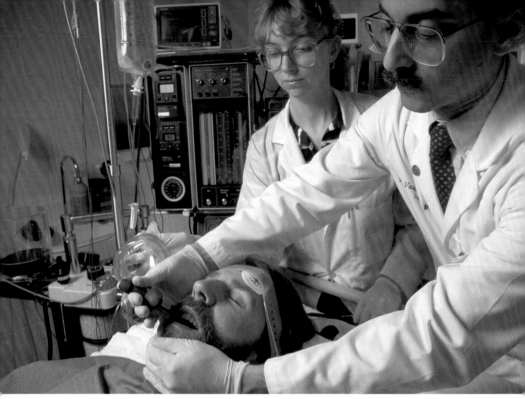

A patient is prepared for electroconvulsive therapy (ECT); the controversial treatment is also known as "shock therapy."

anesthesia, sometimes resulting in permanent memory loss. Seventy-five years after ECT was introduced, it remains controversial. The treatment today is far different; the currents are now precisely calibrated to provide the greatest benefit. ECT has a number of risks and side effects. Some patients say that ECT treatments result in confusion or memory loss, but recent research indicates that it has no long-lasting adverse effects on memory or brain functioning.

ECT usually is used for cases of severe depression accompanied by delusions or hallucinations or in which the person has suicidal or homicidal thoughts or urges. ECT may also be used when a patient with severe depression cannot take antidepressants or has not responded to other treatment options. An estimated 1 million people worldwide receive ECT every year, usually in a course of six to twelve treatments administered two or three times a week.

One of the advantages of ECT over antidepressants is that it typically works much more rapidly. Some patients need only one course of ECT before they feel its benefit. Others may need several courses of ECT over a year or so. Patients undergoing ECT often are prescribed an antidepressant or mood stabilizing medication to supplement the ECT treatments and prevent relapse. Raymond, a twenty-six-year-old, writes that ECT has helped him:

> I've undergone eight ECT treatments in the hospital for severe, suicidal depression where meds alone were not being effective enough. The ECT treatments have totally wiped out the great cloud of depression and suicide that weighed on me for years. I am so much more peaceful now and appreciative of life, especially my own. . . . I still have to take meds but they work much better since I've had ECT and I don't take half as much as I was![21]

Light Therapy

Light therapy, sometimes called phototherapy, is sometimes used to alleviate seasonal affective disorder and some other types of depression by exposure to bright artificial light. During light therapy, the person sits in front of a device called a light therapy box, which mimics natural daylight. Daily exposure to the light is thought to alter or reestablish the body's natural, healthy sleep-wake cycle and suppress the release of melatonin. Together these factors cause biochemical changes in the brain that may help reduce and/or control symptoms of depression.

Light therapy offers an inexpensive and convenient means of treatment with very few side effects. It is often used in conjunction with medication, psychotherapy, or other treatment approaches. For people with seasonal affective disorder, light therapy may be all that is required for full recovery.

Alternative Medicines and Herbal Remedies

A number of alternative medicines have been proposed to treat depression. The most widely used herb is the extract from St.

John's wort (*Hypericum perforatum*), a wildflower considered a weed in most of the United States. Its reputation for
alleviating the symptoms of depression, anxiety, and several
other mood disorders has made St. John's wort one of the best-
selling botanical extracts in the United States.

More than thirty clinical studies have been conducted over
the past two decades to evaluate the effectiveness of St. John's
wort. Results have been mixed. While some scientific evidence
suggests that St. John's wort is helpful in treating mild to moderate depression, two large studies sponsored by the National
Center for Complementary and Alternative Medicine (NCCAM)
showed that the herb was no more effective than a placebo in
treating major depression of moderate severity.

Other remedies suggested by advocates of alternative medicine include S-adenosylmethionine (SAM-E), an amino acid
believed to improve brain chemistry; 5-hydroxytryptophan (5-
HTP), an amino acid that is converted by the brain to serotonin;
ginkgo biloba, an herbal remedy said to improve blood circula-
tion; and Siberian ginseng, which, according to one Web site,
"improves the balance of important neurotransmitters [and]
is believed to stimulate the immune system, enhance abstract
thinking and improve aerobic capacity."[22]

For some people, these remedies are useful in relieving the
symptoms of depression, but it is important to recognize that
herbs are sold as food, not drugs, and are not regulated by the
FDA. In addition, herbal remedies do not require the warnings
of side effects or assurance of research-proven therapeutic
effect. Experts caution that the placebo effect may account
for many of the benefits people claim they have gleaned from
these alternative remedies.

Herbal remedies for depression can be dangerous. Research
has shown that St. John's wort, for instance, can have serious negative side effects and adverse drug interactions. The
FDA cautions that the herb appears to interfere with certain
medications used to treat heart disease, depression, seizures,
certain cancers, and organ transplant rejection. Because 5-HTP
releases serotonin, taking it with other antidepressants can

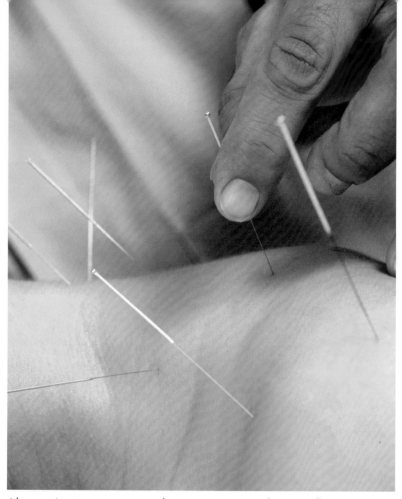

Alternative treatments such as acupuncture (pictured) are gaining in popularity as remedies for the symptoms of depression.

lead to a potentially life-threatening adverse drug reaction called "serotonin syndrome."

Another alternative treatment that has been used for depression is acupuncture. In this two-thousand-year-old procedure, the acupuncturist inserts needles at certain points of the body, acting upon the central nervous system, which then responds by releasing endorphins and immune system cells to promote healing. Some scientists believe that acupuncture may play a role in altering brain chemistry by effecting changes in the release of neurotransmitters and hormones. A 1998 study at the University of Arizona found that 43 percent of participants receiving acupuncture reported a reduction in depressive symptoms compared with just 22 percent in a control group.

Following Through

Not all treatment options are equal. People react uniquely to different drugs, different therapists, and different approaches. Moreover, some medications that appear to work well at the outset of treatment may lose effectiveness. Regardless of the treatment plan, recovery often depends upon ongoing monitoring so that the doctor and patient can change the course of treatment if it is not working.

Depression often may cause and be influenced by coexisting illnesses. Doctors sometimes fail to recognize the impact that other factors have on depression and therefore cannot change the treatment accordingly. In addition, doctors may not continue to monitor patients after they recover from a depressive episode. This can increase the risk of a recurring problem. "Clinicians need to pay particular attention to those patients with chronic depression and identify any co-existing conditions that may be exacerbating the depression or interfering with treatment," says A. John Rush, a research doctor at the University of Texas Southwestern Medical Center. "They need to closely monitor both the symptoms and side effects of these most vulnerable patients throughout treatment and suggest different treatment strategies when needed. Diligent follow-up, even after a patient becomes symptom-free, is essential to avoid relapse."[23]

Many people who are treated for a depressive episode go on to live healthy lives without a recurrence. This is particularly true when a depressive episode is triggered by a specific circumstance. Women with postpartum depression, for instance, typically feel better after a few months, after they have adjusted to their new life and their hormones are back to normal. Similarly, people who suffer a depressive episode triggered by a major life change may be able to be weaned off of antidepressants as their grief subsides or as they adjust to the change. One woman writes on an Internet message board:

> I struggled with some mental health issues for many years, and found relief with anti-depressants and other medications. However, I took these medications [only]

until I felt I could stop. With the help of my doctor, I weaned off the meds and have been able to cope—with the use of tools I found through therapy. . . . [I've been] without anti-depressants for over a year now.[24]

For some people with depression, the illness may be a life-long condition with symptoms that ebb and flow. Hopelessness is common when people are at the darkest depths of depression, but many highly successful people in all walks of life have struggled—and continue to struggle—with the disease. People who have experienced episodes of major depression often learn to recognize the stresses that trigger their depression and how to avoid or cope with such stresses. People with depression also learn to recognize the symptoms of their illness and to seek treatment early on—before the depression becomes serious. They may take antidepressants; engage in psychotherapy; or use exercise, diet, or meditation to fight off the symptoms of depressive illness.

CHAPTER FOUR

Living with Depression

Depression is different for everyone. Some forms of depression are relatively easily treated. About half of all depressed patients experience a single episode and recover completely.

For some, however, depression can be debilitating. For these people a diagnosis of depression is only the beginning of a lifelong treatment plan involving antidepressants and psychotherapy. Even when treated, depression can last for many years. In a 2006 study of patients diagnosed with depression, those who were taking prescription antidepressants had been taking them for an average of 5.5 years, and those in psychotherapy had been in therapy for 5.8 years.

In the deepest periods of depression, people may feel a sense of hopelessness and dread, but those who have recovered are quick to share with others what helped them emerge from their darkest despair and what continues to help them stay one step ahead of the illness. Singer and songwriter Billy Joel, for instance, was hospitalized and received treatment for depression after he tried to commit suicide by drinking furniture polish in the 1970s. Joel later recorded "You're Only Human (Second Wind)" as a message to help prevent teen suicide.

Finding the Right Treatment

Many people diagnosed with depression have felt sad for years without knowing why. A diagnosis of depression is often a relief, although no cure has been found, and treatment usually does not have an immediate effect on symptoms. Some patients do not respond well to their prescribed medication. In a 2006 study more than three-quarters of patients diagnosed with depression reported switching medications at least once, and some patients had tried several different options. Sometimes it takes months or even years to find the best drug or combination of drugs.

This can be frustrating for patients and increase the sense of anger, hopelessness, despair, or other depressive symptoms. "Help!" writes a blogger, "I have been on so many medications it's terrible. Some have not helped at all, some seemed to have worked for a while then just stopped working. My doctors will up the dosages 2 or 3 times before switching me to something else. It is a constant cycle. . . . All I want is to live a normal life, but I think that is too much to ask for."[25]

Patients who have been helped by prescription drugs encourage those who do not respond to a drug right away to keep looking for a solution. Different classes of drugs work differently. One patient says that she has tried many prescription drugs during her ten-year battle with depression. She

Side effects such as stomach cramping and nausea may sometimes occur when taking antidepressant drugs.

encourages others to continue to work with their doctors to find the optimal solution. "Try the SNRI medications if you have not already," she writes. "Compare them with how you felt on strictly SSRIs. You may learn something about your own brain chemistry that can help you select the right antidepressant to defeat your depression once and for all. I know this information has helped me combat mine. . . . Since being on [an SNRI], I feel happier than I have in years."[26]

The Cost of Treatment

Patients with depression are at higher risk than most of giving in to their despair and failing to follow the protocol prescribed by their doctor. If an antidepressant does not seem to be working, patients might try to increase the dosage themselves. More often, however, they simply quit taking it.

For some patients, the cost of treatment may be a problem in itself. Some Americans have no health insurance or have policies that do not cover mental illness. In a 2006 survey of patients with depression, 12 percent of patients who were taking prescription medication for their depression spent more than one hundred dollars per month of their own money on the drugs; 34 percent of those in psychotherapy spent more than one hundred dollars per month on this treatment. This adds to the risk that people will opt out of their treatment. In fact, 23 percent of the patients in the 2006 study said that they were not taking medication for their depression due to cost considerations.

Stigma and Prejudice

Despite the fact that so many people suffer from depression, those afflicted with it are often hesitant to talk about it. Some may be too embarrassed to discuss their emotional problems with a medical professional. Former first lady Barbara Bush told talk show host Larry King that she suffered from depression in the 1970s, likely triggered by her children leaving home and the stress of her husband's career. Looking back on it, Bush regrets not having sought help sooner. "The doctor could have helped me and I was too stupid to go," she told King. "I just didn't want to tell anyone. I mean, I was ashamed of it." [27]

Tipper Gore, the wife of former vice president Al Gore, suffered from depression in the late 1980s, perhaps triggered by her son's tragic automobile accident. She sought help privately—quietly—until she realized that keeping quiet about her experience was adding to the problem. Gore went public with her depression—and the successful treatment she received. She also has sought to reduce the stigma of depression. "Stigma remains the biggest barrier to people getting adequate treatment [for depression]. The good news is there is diagnosis and treatment available. . . . But stigma can cause people to deny what they are seeing in a loved one."[28]

Those diagnosed with depression might avoid telling others about their illness because they fear a negative reaction. This is particularly true in the workplace. In a 2006 survey, the majority of patients told their families (74 percent) and friends (59 percent) about their depression, but only 21 percent shared their diagnosis with coworkers and 11 percent with their employers.

In some cases the fear of what will happen is justified. Friends may not know what to say or how to react. People have lost jobs and promotions because of their illness. In 1972 Senator Thomas Eagleton was pressured to give up his spot as vice presidential candidate on the Democratic ticket with George McGovern after he revealed that he had been treated for depression. In *Depression and Bipolar Disorders* psychiatrist Virginia Edwards tells of a man who was denied mortgage insurance on his home when he answered "yes" to a question asking whether he took antidepressants. She notes that a physical condition such as high blood pressure may lead to a loss of income, but that it is doubtful the man would have been denied insurance coverage for taking blood pressure medication.

"Unfortunately, the term *mental illness* has come to have all kinds of negative connotations," explains Francis Mark Mondimore in *Depression*. "Some of the myths are that people with mental illness are dangerous; that mental illness is untreatable; that the symptoms of mental illness are bizarre and shocking; and that victims of mental illness, indeed their whole families, are somehow cursed or tainted."[29]

The federal Americans with Disabilities Act protects people from being fired because they have a disability, including depression or other mental illness, but their work output is expected to meet their employers' standards. Some depressed people, however, may be unable to meet those standards due to loss of concentration, memory, and decision-making skills. Add to this the amount of sick leave that depressed people may need in order to deal with their symptoms and other associated illnesses, and the reason that so many of them find it difficult to keep their jobs becomes clear.

Many of those who have experienced depression are working with mental health professionals to reduce the stigma. Educating people about the illness may be the first step. ""We need to make sure people can get help for their mental illness without fear of losing their job, recrimination, without being discriminated against," says Tipper Gore. "Most important of all they need the support of their family, friends and colleagues and this can only be achieved if people understand what these biochemical illnesses really are."[30]

The Strain on Day-to-Day Life and Relationships

As depressed patients await a treatment that will help them function, they sometimes no longer find the energy or desire to continue their normal activities. They may drop out of school, quit their job, or find a less demanding job. When they do not have the energy for or interest in activities, their relationships with others might deteriorate and friendships erode. In short, people may find themselves with a diminishing quality of life. "My major depression made me withdraw from everyone and everything," writes a recent college graduate. "I just feel so sad that I missed out on what were supposed to be the best years of my life because of this . . . disease, which just makes me spiral even deeper into a funk."[31]

Depression can strain relationships to the breaking point. People with depression often recognize the toll the disease takes on those around them. In one study, half of all patients with children under eighteen said that their depression had hindered their ability to participate in their children's daily activities and functions.

Family members and friends often agree that living with someone with depression can be trying. In many people the depression manifests itself as moodiness, irritability, forgetfulness, and anxiety. A depressed person may be unpredictable and prone to emotional outbursts of anger or tears. Family members and friends who do not understand that these are

Depression and Suicide

One of the most tragic consequences of depression is the high risk of suicide that goes along with the disorder. Some mental health professionals believe untreated depression to be the largest cause of suicide. Suicide is the eighth leading cause of death in the United States and is the third leading cause of death for fifteen- to twenty-four-year-olds. Almost all people who take their own lives have a diagnosable mental disorder. Suicide rates are higher among people with depression who also drink alcohol or take drugs.

Most suicides occur when the person is recovering from depression, six to nine months after leaving the hospital. Experts speculate that this may be because people with severe depression lack the energy to commit suicide. As people respond to antidepressants or other types of treatment, there may be a period in which they still feel a sense of hopelessness but now have more energy. Close monitoring of severely depressed patients by family, friends, and medical professionals, particularly during the early phases of treatment, can help reduce the risk of suicide.

symptoms of insomnia might take the outbursts personally and respond with anger. Even those who know that a loved one has depression might not know what to do or say. Some people choose to say nothing rather than risk saying the wrong things. Better education about depression and its physical causes can help reduce the stigma and build bridges between a person with depression and his or her loved ones.

The behaviors of some people with depression may also contribute to relationship problems. Depression is often associated with alcohol or drug abuse, which can exacerbate symptoms and lead to violent, unpredictable, or risky behavior. Loved ones may worry about a person with depression, particularly if severe depression seems to interfere with the person's desire to live. Statistics suggest that, at some point, 41 percent of people suffering from depression are suicidal. The threat of suicide can be very unsettling for family members.

Connections with family and community are sometimes all that prevent people from carrying through with suicidal tendencies. "People who have values emphasizing connected-

A woman visits her depressed mother in a nursing home. Close family relationships may reduce the risk of suicide for depressed individuals.

ness to the community are deterred from committing suicide," Edwards explains. "Reasons for living, such as responsibility to family, fear of social or moral disapproval, and strong spirituality, also help to deter people from committing suicide."[32] Experts emphasize the importance of taking talk of suicide seriously and getting help immediately if a person with depression threatens suicide or starts behaving in a manner that causes concern.

Special Problems in Children and Teens

Mental health experts say that treating depression can be particularly challenging when the patient is a child or teenager. First, it is more difficult to diagnose depression in children because many of the symptoms of depression—changes in appetite, moodiness, temper tantrums—are typical of a normal, healthy childhood. In adolescence, too, it can be difficult to tell that something is wrong. Teenagers often sleep until noon, experience changes in appetite, and appear withdrawn, aloof, or emotional.

Experts stress the importance of early diagnosis and treatment of depression in young people, however. Left untreated, teen depression can lead to problems at home and school, drug abuse, self-hatred, risky behavior, and even suicide. Unlike adults, children and teenagers usually depend on parents and other caregivers to get them the help they need.

Mental health professionals suggest that parents should look for signs of depression in their children, particularly if the family has a history of mental illness. Change might signal that something is wrong. Many rebellious and unhealthy behaviors are actually indications of depression. Children with depression may pretend to be sick, refuse to go to school, get in trouble at school, or cling to a parent. Teens sometimes run away or skip school. Eating disorders, substance abuse, and reckless behavior might also point to a problem. An alarming and increasing number of teenagers attempt suicide, and too many succeed. According to the CDC, suicide is the third leading cause of death for fifteen- to twenty-four-year-olds.

How Does Depression Differ in Teens and Adults?

The symptoms of teen depression differ from those of adults, as discussed in this excerpt from "Teen Depression: A Guide for Parents and Teachers," a Web site maintained by the non-profit HELPGUIDE.org, which is dedicated to providing information that empowers people to take charge of their own health.

Depression in teens can look very different from depression in adults. The following symptoms of depression are more common in teenagers than in their adult counterparts:

- **Irritable or angry mood**—Irritability, rather than sadness, is often the predominant mood in depressed teens. A depressed teenager may be grumpy, hostile, easily frustrated, or prone to angry outbursts.
- **Unexplained aches and pains**—Depressed teens frequently complain about physical ailments such as headaches or stomachaches. If a thorough physical exam does not reveal a medical cause, these aches and pains may indicate depression.
- **Extreme sensitivity to criticism**—Depressed teens are plagued by feelings of worthlessness, making them extremely vulnerable to criticism, rejection, and failure. This is particularly a problem for "over-achievers."
- **Withdrawing from some but not all people**—While adults tend to isolate themselves when depressed, teenagers usually keep up at least some friendships. However, teens with depression may socialize less than before, pull away from their parents, or start hanging out with a different crowd.

Experts emphasize the importance of getting help for troubled youth right away. When dealing with a child who has depression, parents and other family members have to balance the need to maintain appropriate discipline with an open attitude that encourages their children to talk about their problems. Talking about depression can be difficult. Getting through to one's child can be a challenge. Living with a depressed teenager can be draining. When a teen acts out, family members are tempted to believe that he or she is being difficult on purpose. In addition to the stress any family member feels when dealing with a depressed loved one, many parents feel a sense of guilt, loss, and sadness when they see their children suffering.

Treatment options also can be tricky. Teens cannot get treatment on their own; they often have to first admit their feelings to a parent or other trusted adults. Some teens may be unwilling to talk to "strangers" about their feelings. Still, countless young people have benefited from psychotherapy. Mental health professionals can be instrumental in diagnosing depression and getting teens the help they need. An experienced mental health counselor can help teens understand their feelings and problems and learn how to deal with them in their everyday life. Young people may be more willing to talk about their problems and emotions with a concerned and knowledgeable professional than they are with a parent or even a close friend. Teens often benefit from realizing that they are not alone—that many others are going through the difficulties they are experiencing.

Medical professionals may prescribe drugs for teens with serious depression, but drug therapy is more complicated for young people than for adults. Experts have raised serious concerns about the use of antidepressants for teens. "The human brain is developing exponentially when we are very young," says Amir Raz, a neuroscientist who has studied the impact of antidepressants on teens, "and exposure to antidepressants may affect or influence the wiring of the brain, especially when it comes to certain elements that have to do with stress,

Depressed teens often find it difficult to open up about their feelings, which may cause them to withdraw from friends and family.

emotion, and the regulation of these."[33] Antidepressant medications also have become associated with suicide in teens, earning them a "black box" warning label from the U.S. Food and Drug Administration. Still, antidepressants have helped many teens who are thought to be at risk of suicide unless they get immediate help.

Coping Mechanisms

Outside of medical treatment, having a strong network of family and friends is perhaps the most important predictor of whether a person will recover from depression and its symptoms. Fortunately, many support groups can help people with depression and their families. Support groups share information about the disease and offer personal insight into treatment options and coping techniques. Some depression support groups are sponsored by nonprofit health care organizations or local government agencies; others meet informally.

Support groups that meet over the Internet may be particularly helpful to people with severe depression or who fear a new situation. Internet support groups also have the advantage of allowing for anonymity, which may help those who worry about the stigma of mental illness. For some people, local groups that enable people with depression to make connections with one another and reduce the sense of isolation may be important aspects of a treatment plan. Support groups also can help family members adjust to living with a person with depression.

Some experts say that maintaining a positive attitude is the most important thing people can do. Depressed individuals are not likely to "snap out of it," but therapists say such people can take steps to convince themselves that they feel better. Severely depressed people might need to set small, realistic goals for themselves, such as getting out of bed or bathing. Other goals might focus on activities the person used to enjoy, such as seeing a friend or going to a movie, ballgame, or other event. One of the dangers of depression is the isolation that results; experts emphasize the importance of maintaining relationships with others.

Depression saps a person's energy. For this reason, it is important to break up large tasks into small ones and to set priorities in order to experience a sense of accomplishment. Experts also emphasize the importance of being nice to oneself.

Many people believe that the best treatment for depression is a healthy lifestyle. A well-balanced diet and moderate daily exercise can help prevent a depressive state from deepening.

How Friends and Family Can Help

The first and most important thing that can be done to help a friend or relative who has depression is to help him or her get an appropriate diagnosis and treatment. This may entail making an appointment on behalf of the depressed person and going with him or her to see the doctor. This person should be encouraged to stay in treatment or to seek different treatment if no improvement occurs after several weeks.

A better understanding of depression and its symptoms can help people offer support and encouragement to loved ones suffering from depression. Experts emphasize the importance of patience. It is common for those with depression to be irritable or lethargic.

Perhaps the best way a friend can help is to spend time with someone who is depressed. One-on-one time might be all someone with depression needs to open up about his or her feelings and fears. It may be easier for a person with depression to leave the house or go for a walk in the company of others. Even if a person does not want to talk about the illness, it can be good therapy simply to spend time with a supportive friend. Although a friend cannot and should not try to "play therapist," a good friend can be a sounding board and model a positive attitude to a person who is depressed. Perhaps most important is to watch for signs of suicide. Many people contemplating suicide comment on it—sometimes in a joking manner. Experts emphasize the importance of taking suicide threats seriously by reporting such conversations to a relative or professional.

Making lifestyle changes and adopting a healthy regime can be an integral part of treatment.

While few studies explore the relationship between exercise and depression, some researchers believe that regular exercise and improved physical fitness alter serotonin levels in the brain, leading to improved mood and feelings of well-being. Regular exercise also boosts body temperature, which may ease depression by influencing the levels of brain chemicals. In addition, physical activity burns up stress chemicals such as adrenaline and promotes a more relaxed state of mind.

Research suggests that even moderate exercise can help in mild to moderate cases of depression. "I chose to cease SSRI medication four years ago and rely upon [other] strategies to maintain my wellness," writes one depression patient. "In my case, the benefits of a daily 30 to 40 minute [exercise] session within an hour of waking have been measurable, including an increase of energy, elevated mood, and motivation."[34]

In a 2006 study conducted by researchers from the University of Texas, for instance, moderate physical activity such as a brisk thirty-minute walk was shown to ease depressive symptoms. While the effect was almost immediate, researchers are

Attending support group sessions enables people with depression to connect with others, reducing their feelings of isolation.

quick to emphasize that exercise is a short-term solution for the symptoms of depression, not a cure for the disease itself.

Aside from the physical impact on depression, exercise may benefit patients in other ways. Some forms of exercise may serve as a social event. Participating in a weekly exercise class or joining a team sport might help reduce feelings of isolation. An enjoyable period of exercise might be distracting enough to break the vicious cycle of pessimistic thinking, and simply taking a more active role in one's own recovery can be a boost to self-esteem.

Diet and Nutrition

Vitamin deficiencies may contribute to symptoms associated with depression. For instance, the B-complex vitamins are essential to mental and emotional well-being. The body cannot store them, so people depend entirely on their daily diets for an adequate supply. In addition, B vitamins are destroyed by alcohol, refined sugars, nicotine, and caffeine. Some people who experience anxiety, stress, or other symptoms associated with depression try to relax with a cigarette, binge on food, or self-medicate with alcohol, so it is no surprise that many people with depression may be deficient in B vitamins.

Similarly, deficiencies in a number of minerals, including magnesium, zinc, iron, and potassium, can cause exhaustion, lethargy, and lack of appetite. A calcium deficiency has been shown to affect the central nervous system, causing nervousness, apprehension, irritability, and numbness. For these reasons, many experts believe that a properly balanced diet may be a key element of a depression treatment plan.

It is also important for patients to eat enough protein to maintain skin, organ, muscle, and immune function. Recent research suggests that one particular component of protein, the amino acid tryptophan, is important in its effect on the brain, where it influences mood. Tryptophan can be added to the diet by ensuring that at least one type of protein is eaten at each meal—fish, meat, eggs, milk, cheese, nuts, beans, lentils, or tofu.

Experts also emphasize the importance of sleep. In fact, some studies show that inadequate sleep may cause depression. Learning stress reduction techniques may be helpful in reducing depression. Some people find yoga, meditation, and breathing techniques helpful. These strategies date back to ancient Asian philosophies and help people focus on the present moment. Therapists working with depressed patients sometimes use meditation or relaxation techniques to help patients change the way they react to situations and manage their feelings. These techniques can help relieve stress by helping people accept what cannot be changed.

Stability is important. Establishing a routine will enable depressed people to learn what works for them, how they can minimize the symptoms of the illness, and how to recognize the warning signs that a depressive episode is getting worse. The path to recovery requires patients to keep appointments with their doctors and other mental health professionals, follow their doctors' advice, and take medications as prescribed. It also requires patients to be willing to talk about their moods and feelings. Building support networks of family, friends, and others who understand what depressed patients are going through can be critical. Some people also find that taking notes on what is happening at school or work, as well as on sleep, eating, and exercise patterns, can help identify stressors that may trigger or increase depressive symptoms. Finally, education is important because it allows patients to make informed decisions about treatment and to feel as much in control as possible of their depression and its symptoms.

CHAPTER FIVE

New Findings and Solutions

Although scientists have learned a great deal about depression over the past several decades, they are quick to point out that much remains unknown. Research shows a link between neurotransmitters such as serotonin and mood, for instance, but scientists are not sure exactly how SSRIs and other antidepressants affect these neurotransmitters. Scientists are also working to gain greater understanding of the causes and diagnosing of depression.

The number of drugs and classes of drugs available to treat depression has grown exponentially. While new classes of drugs provide relief for millions of people, scientists disagree about the safety and effectiveness of commonly prescribed medications. Research has not shown conclusively what happens to neurotransmitters when antidepressants are taken, and some scientists are skeptical about whether the vast majority of patients truly need the drugs they have been prescribed.

While many people who are taking the drugs may not need them, millions of people with depression are not being treated. Many people do not recognize the signs or symptoms of depression; in many of those who do, the depression may be mistaken for another problem. Even when properly diagnosed, not all patients with depression are helped through treatment. For some, the side effects of current drugs are worse than the depression itself; for others, the drugs simply do not alleviate the depression.

A psychologist at the Menninger Clinic in Houston, Texas, writes, "To summarize the problem: depressed persons may not realize that they're ill; if they do recognize it, they may not seek treatment; if they do seek treatment, they may not be diagnosed; if they are diagnosed, they may be under-treated; if they are adequately treated, they may not fully respond; and if they do respond, they may experience a recurrence."[35] All of these factors point to the need for a new and better understanding of the disease, as well as diagnosis and treatment options.

Diagnosis

Some experts are critical of current approaches to diagnosing depression and emphasize that additional research is needed to improve the current diagnostic tools. Studies have suggested that too many doctors, particularly general practitioners, prescribe antidepressants to patients who do not need them. Depression-like symptoms are common in people who have been through a stressful experience such as a divorce or natural disaster. Some scientists warn that antidepressant drugs are being used to "treat" these symptoms, which are in fact natural or normal reactions to stress. Jerome Wakefield, who led a 2007 study of depression, warned that using a checklist of symptoms to diagnose depression is insufficient and that doctors do not pay enough attention to the circumstances involved. "The cost of not looking at context is you think anyone who comes under this diagnosis has a biological disorder, so should more or less automatically get antidepressant medication, and everything else is superfluous," writes Wakefield. "There is a trend to treat people in this somewhat mechanized way."[36] Several studies are looking at improving the diagnostic tools used by professionals to add components that would help differentiate between people who are reacting to stress and those who are truly depressed.

In the future scientists might be able to use magnetic resonance imaging (MRI) and other imaging methods as diagnostic

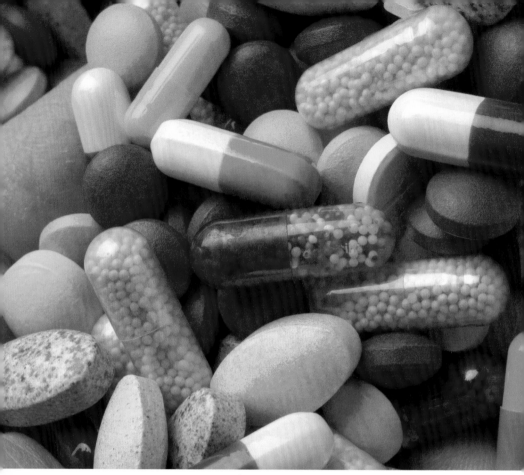

Many scientists question the safety and effectiveness of the large number of drugs available to treat depression.

tools for depression. Early studies comparing the brain of a person with depression to those of a "normal" person suggest that there are important differences. For instance, the hippocampus of depressed patients, which regulates emotion and memory, tends to be smaller. In addition, images of the brains of bipolar patients show an unusual number of bright spots in some of the regions involved in mood, including the thalamus, basal ganglia, and brain stem. One recent study suggested that increased activity in the amygdala of the left hemisphere might indicate heightened vulnerability to future depression. Improvements in imaging technology might also make it possible to examine the concentrations of neurotransmitters, so that densities of those molecules can be compared in different people and in various areas of the brain.

Researchers are especially concerned about improving diagnostic techniques for the elderly, children, and adolescents. Symptoms of depression among the elderly are often believed to be signs of aging or mistaken for dementia. In children and teens, the symptoms can resemble attention-deficit hyperactivity disorder (ADHD) or other illnesses, or may be overlooked as a normal part of adolescence. When teens turn to drugs or alcohol, the treatment focuses on weaning them off of these substances without addressing the underlying depression. Studies that use high-tech imaging to identify brain activity can help distinguish depression from other ailments, enabling quicker, more accurate diagnoses for at-risk populations.

Research into Causes

A great deal of research is being conducted into the various causes of depression. One area of investigation involves questions about why depression is more prevalent and why its onset is happening at younger and younger ages. One theory is that depression is being diagnosed more effectively in children and teens, but some scientists believe that more children and teens are actually suffering from the illness than in previous generations.

Researchers are also investigating the many causes of depression in an effort to determine how the contributing factors interrelate. Studies looking at seasonal affective disorder and other types of depression in different parts of the world are helping to provide a glimpse into the role that the environment—specifically light—plays in depression. Just as too little light appears to contribute to some kinds of depression, too much light at night may also contribute to the problem. In a 2009 study of mice in a laboratory setting, for instance, researchers reported that mice exposed to constant light showed depressive symptoms not shown by those who had more natural cycles of daylight.

Scientists are also looking at how life events, stress, thought patterns, and personality affect the onset of depression. Looking at family histories and the pattern that depression takes in one individual's life can help researchers to better understand the factors that might lead to recurring episodes.

Researchers would also like to learn more about the role that sexual, physical, and emotional abuse plays in depression. Studies suggest a link between childhood abuse and neglect and adult depression. One recent study compared the experi-

Scientists are investigating the reasons that depression is occurring in children at younger and younger ages.

ence of patients who had suffered abuse as children with those who had not. The study found that those who had been abused as children tended to become depressed at a younger age, have more severe symptoms, were more likely to "self-medicate" through drugs and alcohol, and were more likely to attempt suicide.

The role of genetics is also the subject of a great deal of research. Scientists believe that a genetic component contributes to depression and are conducting research to identify the gene or genes that may carry the disease. Some researchers are studying the DNA of people in families with two or more members who have depression in an attempt to figure out which gene or genes might make people more susceptible to the disease and its symptoms.

Some scientists are studying the impact of a gene called corticotrophin-releasing hormone receptor one (CRHR1), which controls the body's response to stress hormones. In one recent study of people who had suffered child abuse, those who carried the most protective form of the gene had markedly lower measures of depression.

Scientists also believe they have identified a gene, TREK-1, that can affect transmission of serotonin in the brain. In one study, scientists bred mice with an absence of this gene and then tested them using a range of measures known to gauge depression. Although the research is still in its infancy, scientists hope that the study of these genes might lead to a new generation of antidepressants.

Another area of research focuses on the structure of the brain itself. Recent studies suggest that in cases of familial depression, changes in tissue thickness in key brain structures in the right half of the brain may increase a person's risk for developing depression. Similar changes in the left half of the brain were linked to the severity of a person's existing depression or anxiety symptoms. More research is needed to determine if the inherited risk for depression is purely genetic, if specific environmental factors trigger genetic predisposition, or whether a combination of factors is involved.

Brain Imaging Techniques

Scientists are comparing the brains of depressed and nonde-pressed people to learn whether differences in the structure of the brain might be a contributing factor to depression. Many of these studies rely on brain-imaging technologies.

One of the technologies often used to study the brain is mag-netic resonance imaging (MRI). The MRI machine is essentially a giant scanner. A horizontal tube runs through the machine from front to back. The patient, lying on his or her back, slides into the tube. The scan uses a magnetic field with radio wave pulses of energy to build a map of tissue types. It then integrates this information into a 2-D or 3-D image, providing an unparalleled view of the inside of the human body.

In researching the causes of depression, scientists use magnetic resonance imaging (MRI) to examine a depressed patient's brain structure.

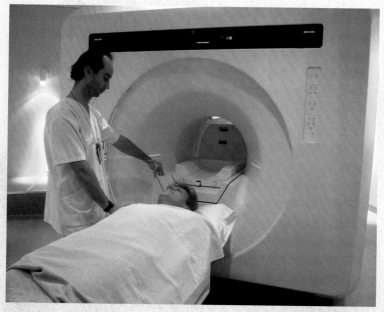

Other researchers are studying brain chemistry to learn more about the abnormalities that may contribute to depression. Studies have found that the function of serotonin is abnormal in people with depression, but scientists have little conclusive evidence about what causes the abnormality.

Research into Treatment

Much of the research on depression focuses on treatment options. Of particular concern to many researchers is the treatment of depression in children and teens, who do not always respond as well as adults to traditional treatment strategies. Experts have long believed that successfully addressing depression in young people may be the key to avoiding later serious bouts of the illness. In addition, interest in addressing depression among young people has also grown in response to serious concerns about prescribing antidepressants to young people. Closely monitored clinical trials also are being undertaken to explore the link between antidepressants and suicidal thoughts in teens. Scientists also are studying how antidepressant medications affect the developing brain in the hope of developing safer options for teenage patients. Researchers are exploring some of the differences between teens and adults to learn more about how to craft treatment plans that address the specific needs of teens. Researchers are especially concerned about teens' higher risk of suicide and their inability to seek treatment on their own. Researchers also are looking at the long-term effectiveness of psychotherapy and medication on teen depression and on the factors that influence recovery.

A number of other treatment options are still in the experimental phase. One such treatment, called transcranial magnetic stimulation, or TMS, involves applying powerful electromagnets directly to the skull. TMS is based on the realization that electrical activity on the left side of the brain where mood is controlled is diminished in depressed patients. TMS uses electromagnets to send pulses of energy directly into this side of the brain, creating an electric current and getting the brain cells to fire. "One can think of this as sort of getting a jumper cable and jump-starting your car because your battery has been drained,"[37] says neurologist Alvaro Pascual-Leone, who has used TMS at Beth Israel Deaconess Medical Center in Boston.

TMS is still in the research phase. The FDA has not approved it for widespread use, but preliminary results are promising. One of the advantages, say researchers, is that it is a safe and painless procedure. Patients are generally treated for a few weeks and, if it works, the depression is staved off for months at a time.

Another experimental treatment for chronic depression is vagus nerve stimulation (VNS, also called vagal nerve stimu-

A woman with powerful electromagnets affixed to her head undergoes a transcranial magnetic stimulation (TMS) treatment.

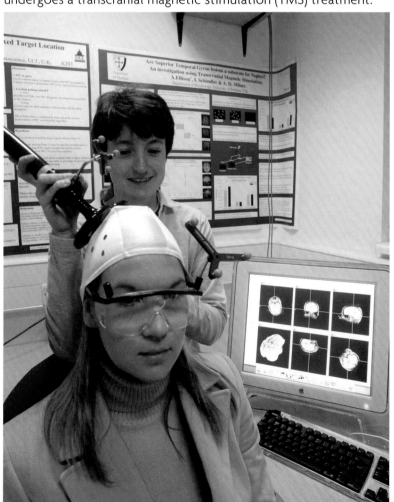

National Institute of Mental Health

The National Institute of Mental Health (NIMH) is one of the world's leading mental health biomedical organizations. The mission of NIMH is to transform the understanding and treatment of mental illnesses through basic and clinical research, paving the way for prevention, recovery, and cure.

NIMH researchers are involved in a wide range of studies on the causes, diagnosis, prevention, and treatment of depression in the United States. Some of this research is done in-house, but the NIMH also provides grants to support research at universities, hospitals, and other research institutions throughout the United States and the world.

The NIMH is working with scientists in different disciplines to use the tools of molecular and cellular biology, genetics, epidemiology, and cognitive and behavioral science to better understand the factors that influence brain function and behavior, including mental illness. The NIMH is particularly focused on research that will help scientists work together to translate research in the laboratory to real-world uses.

lation). VNS involves implanting a small device in the neck, where the vagus nerve is located. The device sends electrical impulses along the vagus nerve into the brain. These signals affect the mood centers of the brain. Vagus nerve stimulation has been used to treat epilepsy since 1997, and the FDA approved its use for depression in 2005 but only for chronic recurrent or severe depression that has not responded to other treatments. Although early studies researching the impact of VNS on depression are inconclusive, some scientists believe it may gain acceptance as it is proven to work in treatment-resistant cases of depression.

Research into Drugs

Antidepressants such as Prozac and Paxil have made pharmaceutical companies billions of dollars, so it is no surprise that drug companies are constantly involved in researching potential drugs. Drug testing is a long and cumbersome process, however. Chemical compounds are first tried in a lab and then tested on animals. Only after years of testing to ensure that a potential remedy is safe can it be used on people in clinical trials.

One drug in clinical trials is moclobemide (trade name Moclamine). Developed by Roche, this is a short-acting and reversible MAO inhibitor that has been shown to increase brain levels of serotonin and noradrenaline. Research suggests that the compound might prove as effective as SSRIs and TCAs with fewer side effects and lower risks of adverse interaction with foods.

Some drug research is focused on targeting new areas of the brain. Researchers from the University of Iowa found that disrupting ASIC1a—a brain protein involved in fear and anxiety—produced an antidepressant-like effect in mice. The effect was similar to that produced by currently available antidepressant drugs, but the team believes that it may open a new option for people who do not respond to the current medications. "We need antidepressants with new mechanisms of action to help those people who don't respond to what is currently available,"[38] explains John Wemmie, a psychiatrist and neurologist who worked on the research. Matthew Coryell, the study's lead author, adds, "Because the ASIC1a protein is especially abundant in areas of the brain that regulate emotion, it is possible that interventions targeting ASIC1a could treat depression while having fewer effects on other brain areas and thus fewer side effects than available treatments."[39]

Hope for the Future

The goal of depression research is to better understand the causes of depression and to find new, more effective, and

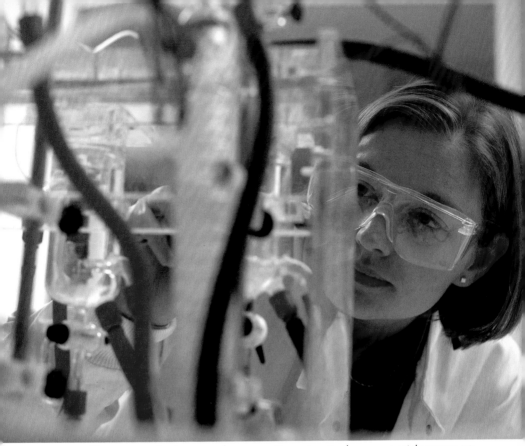

Pharmaceutical researchers continue to study new antidepressant drugs to help in the fight against depression.

safer treatments. While in the past, people had to simply live with depression and its debilitating symptoms, today a number of treatment options are available, and tomorrow will bring still more. Pharmaceutical companies are constantly developing more effective drugs with fewer side effects. And as scientists and doctors are learning more about depression and its causes, treatment is becoming increasingly tailored to the unique needs of the patient. Researchers have a long way to go toward understanding depression, but patients have reason to hope that the darkest days of depression are behind them.

Notes

Introduction: Beyond Sadness

1. Bonnie, "How Depression Feels," Depression.com. www
   .depression.com/types_of_depression.html.
2. Bernard, telephone interview by author, May 18, 2009.

Chapter One: What Is Depression?

3. Quoted in ContactMusic.com, "Sheryl Crow: Sheryl
   Crow's Positive Battle Against Depression," October 14,
   2003. www.contactmusic.com/new/xmlfeed.nsf/story/
   sheryl-crow.s-positive-battle-against-depression.
4. Virginia Edwards, *Depression and Bipolar Disorders:
   Everything You Need to Know*. Buffalo: Firefly, 2002,
   p. 21.
5. Quoted in Ben Cook, "Interview with Barbara Hambly,"
   Andromeda Spaceways Inflight Magazine, December 25,
   2005. www.andromedaspaceways.com/inter_0002.htm.
6. Brooke Shields, *Down Came the Rain: My Journey
   Through Postpartum Depression*. New York: Hyperion,
   2006, p. 55.
7. Shields, *Down Came the Rain*, p. 71.
8. Shields, *Down Came the Rain*, p. 74.
9. Conrad Schwartz and Edward Shorter, *Psychotic Depression*. New York: Cambridge University Press, 2007, pp.
   81–82.
10. Bipolar Disorder Today, "What Bipolar Disorder Feels
    Like." www.mental-health-today.com/bp/art11.htm.
11. Quoted in Bonnie Butterfield, "The Troubled Life of
    Vincent Van Gogh," 1998. http://cvc.csusb.edu/Vincent
    VanGogh.htm.
12. Quoted in Butterfield, "The Troubled Life of Vincent Van
    Gogh."
13. Mary Ellen Copeland, "Coming Out of the Mire," Work-
    place Options/Care Topics: Depression. www.helphorizons
    .com/care/search_details.htm?id=237.

Chapter Two: Causes of Depression

14. John M. Grohol and the National Institute of Mental Health, "Research on Depression," PsychCentral.com, November 7, 2005. http://psychcentral.com/disorders/depressionresearch.htm.

15. Quoted in *ScienceDaily*, "Alcohol Abuse May Lead to Depression Risk, Rather than Vice Versa," March 7, 2009. www.sciencedaily.com/releases/2009/03/090302183002.htm.

Chapter Three: Treatment for Depression

16. Quoted in Rebecca Leung, "Carrey: 'Life Is Too Beautiful," *60 Minutes*, November 21, 2004. www.cbsnews.com/stories/2004/11/18/60minutes/main656547.shtml.

17. Quoted in Leung, "Carrey."

18. Linda, interview by author, May 14, 2009.

19. Quoted in John Morgan, "Terry Bradshaw's Winning Drive Against Depression," *USA Today*, January 30, 2004. www.usatoday.com/news/health/spotlighthealth/2004-01-30-bradshaw_x.htm.

20. B.K. Eakman, "Anything That Ails You," *Chronicles*, August 2004, pp. 20–21.

21. Quoted in ECT.org, "Famous Shock Patients." ECT.org. www.ect.org/famous-shock-patients.

22. Depression-guide.com, "Treating Depression Naturally: Herbal Treatment," 2005. www.depression-guide.com/herbal-remedy-for-depression.htm.

23. Quoted in National Institute of Mental Health: Science Update, "Odds of Beating Depression Diminish as Additional Treatment Strategies Are Needed," November 1, 2006. www.nimh.nih.gov/science-news/2006/odds-of-beating-depression-diminish-as-additional-treatment-strategies-are-needed.shtml.

24. Anonymous, posted at "Weight Loss Since Anti-depressants," PEERtrainer, July 12, 2006. www.peertrainer.com/Lounge CommunityThread.aspx?ForumID=1&ThreadID=24397.

Chapter Four: Living with Depression

25. Anonymous, posted on "Depression: Forum," About.com, May 5, 2009. http://forums.about.com/n/pfx/forum.aspx?tsn=1&nav=messages&webtag=ab-depression&tid=23083.

26. ScribusMedicus, "How Antidepressants Have Helped Me and My Family," Helium. www.helium.com/items/610203-how-antidepressants-have-helped-me-and-my-family.

27. Quoted in *Larry King Live Weekend*, "Barbara Bush Reflects on Her Life as First Lady," January 28, 2001, CNN.com Transcripts. http://transcripts.cnn.com/TRANSCRIPTS/0101/28/lklw.00.html.

28. Quoted in John Morgan, "Tipper Gore Honors Mental Health Achievements," DrDonnica.com. http://www.drdonnica.com/celebrities/00006388.htm.

29. Francis Mark Mondimore, *Depression: The Mood Disease*, 3rd ed. Baltimore: Johns Hopkins University Press, 2006.

30. Quoted in Morgan, "Tipper Gore Honors Mental Health Achievements."

31. Quoted in Carolyn Hax Advice Column, *Washington Post*, May 9, 2009. www.washingtonpost.com/wp-dyn/content/article/2009/05/08/AR2009050803362.html?sub=AR.

32. Edwards, *Depression and Bipolar Disorders*, p. 147.

33. Amir Raz, "Kids on Meds: Trouble Ahead," *Scientific American*, June 2007. www.scientificamerican.com/article.cfm?id=kids-on-meds-trouble-ahead.

34. Quoted in Depresion-Guide.com, "What People Are Saying About Depression-Guide.com." www.depression-guide.com/index.htm.

Chapter Five: New Findings and Solutions

35. Jon G. Allen, "Coping with Depression," Menninger Clinic. www.menningerclinic.com/resources/Depression05.htm.

36. Quoted in Shankar Vedantam, "Criteria for Depression Are Too Broad, Researchers Say," *Washington Post*, April 3, 2007, p. A02.

37. Quoted in Dan Harris, "A New Treatment for Depression: Magnets," ABC News, May 17, 2005. http://abcnews.go.com/WNT/Depression/Story?id=765933&page=1.

38. Quoted in Rick Nauert, "A New Treatment Strategy for Depression," PsychCentral, April 30, 2009. http://psychcentral.com/news/2009/04/30/a-new-treatment-strategy-for-depression/5616.html.

39. Quoted in Nauert, "A New Treatment Strategy for Depression."

Glossary

antidepressants: Prescription medications that may be used to help treat depression.

anxiety: A state of heightened worry, uneasiness, or apprehension.

bipolar disorder: Also called manic depression, this disorder involves periods of extreme elation and energy highs countered with extreme sadness and hopelessness, often with periods of normal feelings between these extremes.

chronic: Long-lasting; always present or occurring over and over.

clinical depression: *See* major depression.

depression: A medical illness characterized by an ongoing feeling of hopelessness and despair, usually combined with poor concentration, lack of energy, and sleep problems.

dopamine: A neurotransmitter that researchers have linked to depression.

dysthymia: Also called dysthymic disorder, a type of depression characterized by moods that are consistently low over a long period of time.

genetic: Inherited from parents, the passing on of physical and behavioral traits.

hormone: Chemical produced by an endocrine gland that regulates body processes such as growth, sleep, and digestion.

insomnia: A medical condition characterized by sleeplessness or poor quality of sleep.

magnetic resonance imaging (MRI): A scan producing an image of the brain or other body part by mapping magnetic fields.

major depression: Also known as major depressive disorder or clinical depression, this mood disorder is characterized by feelings of intense sadness, irritability, changes in appetite and sleep, low self-esteem or self-worth, and feelings of hopelessness and despair.

melancholia: A term used many years ago to describe depression and its symptoms.

mood: A sustained period of emotion.

neurotransmitter: A molecule responsible for transmission of a nerve impulse across the synapse between two nerve cells.

norepinephrine: A neurotransmitter that researchers have linked to depression.

postpartum depression: A type of depression affecting new mothers.

psychiatrist: A medical doctor with training in the diagnosis and treatment of mental and emotional illnesses.

psychologist: A professional who studies behavior and experience, and who is licensed to provide therapeutic services.

psychotherapy: Also called talk therapy; a form of treatment in which a psychiatrist, psychologist, or counselor works to help resolve a patient's mental issues.

psychotic depression: A disorder when a severe depressive illness is accompanied by some form of psychosis, such as hearing voices or having delusions or hallucinations.

seasonal affective disorder (SAD): A type of depression characterized by the onset of a depressive illness during the winter months, when there is less sunlight.

selective serotonin reuptake inhibitors (SSRIs): A class of antidepressant medications that helps the body use serotonin more effectively.

serotonin: A neurotransmitter that researchers have linked to depression.

trauma: Injury or stress caused by an outside force that may have long-lasting psychological effects.

Organizations to Contact

American Psychiatric Association

1000 Wilson Blvd., Ste. 1825

Arlington, VA 22209

phone: (703) 907-7300

e-mail: apa@psych.org

Web site: www.apapsych.org

The American Psychiatric Association is a membership organization with more than 38,000 psychiatrists and other physicians working to ensure effective diagnosis and treatment for people with mental disorders, including depression. The organization engages in a wide range of research and education activities.

American Psychological Association (APA)

750 First St. NE

Washington, DC 20002

phone: (800) 374-2721

Web site: www.apa.org

The APA is a scientific and professional organization that represents psychologists in the United States. With 150,000 members, the APA is the largest association of psychologists worldwide. The mission of the APA is to advance the creation, communication, and application of psychological knowledge to benefit society and improve people's lives.

Depression and Bipolar Support Alliance (DBSA)

730 N. Franklin St., Ste. 501

Chicago, IL 60610

phone: (800) 826-3632
Web site: www.dbsalliance.org

Founded in 1985, the DBSA is a patient-directed national nonprofit organization that conducts research on mood disorders, provides support for those suffering from these disorders and their families, educates the public, and lobbies on behalf of people living with mood disorders. The DBSA has a grassroots network of nearly one thousand patient-run support groups across the country.

Families for Depression Awareness

385 Totten Pond Rd., Ste. 404
Waltham, MA 02451
phone: (781) 890-0220
Web site: www.familyaware.org

Families for Depression Awareness is a national nonprofit organization that helps families and friends recognize and cope with depressive disorders to get people well and prevent suicides. The organization provides education, outreach, and advocacy to support families. Families for Depression Awareness is made up of families who have lost a family member to suicide or have watched a loved one suffer with depression.

Mental Health America

2000 N. Beauregard St.
Alexandria, VA 22311
phone: (800) 969-6642
Web site: www.nmha.org

Mental Health America (formerly known as the National Mental Health Association) is the country's leading nonprofit organization dedicated to helping people live mentally healthier lives. With more than 320 affiliates nationwide, the organization seeks to promote mental wellness by educating the public; fighting for access to effective care; fostering innovation in research, practice, services, and policy; and providing support to more than 60 million individuals and families living with mental health and substance abuse problems.

National Alliance on Mental Illness (NAMI)
2107 Wilson Blvd.
Arlington, VA 22201-3042
phone: (703) 524-7600
Web site: www.nami.org.

NAMI is a grassroots mental health advocacy organization. Since it began in 1979, NAMI has engaged in a wide range of support, awareness and education, advocacy, and research programs to improve the lives of individuals and families affected by mental illness.

National Institute of Mental Health (NIMH)
6001 Executive Blvd.
Bethesda, MD 20892-9663
phone: (301) 443-4513 or (866) 615-6464
Web site: www.nimh.nih.gov

The mission of NIMH, which is part of the National Institutes of Health, is to transform the understanding and treatment of mental illnesses through basic and clinical research, paving the way for prevention, recovery, and cure. The organization offers a breadth of research on and information about diagnosis, causes, and treatment of depression.

For Further Reading

Books

Jon Allen, *Coping with Depression: From Catch-22 to Hope*. Washington, DC: American Psychiatric, 2005. This book addresses the challenges depressed patients face on the road to recovery, focusing particular attention on the importance of hope.

Neil T. Anderson, *Stomping Out Depression*. New York: Regal, 2001. Written for teens with depression and their families, this book discusses the causes and symptoms of depression in teens and preteens and offers a Christian-based approach to its treatment and recovery.

Karen K. Brees, *The Everything Health Guide to Depression*. Avon, MA: Adams Media, 2008. This comprehensive book, written for people suffering from depression, provides information about symptoms, causes, treatment, and research into the illness.

Beverly Cobain, *When Nothing Matters Anymore: A Survival Guide for Depressed Teens*. Minneapolis: Free Spirit, 2007. Written by a cousin of Kurt Cobain, who committed suicide at the age of twenty-seven, this book is intended to help teens recognize the signs of depression and get much-needed help.

Helen A. Demetriades, *Bipolar Disorder, Depression, and Other Mood Disorders*. Berkeley Heights, NJ: Enslow, 2002. Written by a psychologist, this book identifies the cause, symptoms, and treatment of various mood disorders.

Virginia Edwards, *Depression and Bipolar Disorders: Everything You Need to Know*. Buffalo: Firefly, 2002. Written by a psychiatrist, this book describes the difference between "low moods" and depressive disorders, explains how depression affects the brain, and provides insights into treatment options.

Francis Mark Mondimore, *Depression: The Mood Disease*. 3rd ed. Baltimore: Johns Hopkins University Press, 2006. Written by a psychiatrist, this book explains the causes, symptoms, and treatment for various types of depression, and the research currently being undertaken on the disease.

Brooke Shields, *Down Came the Rain: My Journey Through Postpartum Depression*. New York: Hyperion, 2006. Shields's candid memoir describes the depth of the despair that can result from depression.

Faye Zucker and Joan E. Huebl, *Beating Depression: Teens Find Light at the End of the Tunnel*. New York: Franklin Watts, 2007. Written for teens, this book offers statistics about the scope of teen depression, as well as causes, signs and symptoms, and treatment options. The stories of teens help to make the book relevant for a teen audience.

Internet Sources and Web Sites

Neal Conan and Joanne Silberner, "History of Treating Depression," *Talk of the Nation*, NPR, March 25, 2004. www.npr .org/templates/story/story.php?storyId=1791832.

Depression and Bipolar Support Alliance, "About Mood Disorders." www.dbsalliance.org/site/PageServer?pagename= about_MDOverview.

———, "Helping Someone with a Mood Disorder." www.dbs alliance.org/site/PageServer?pagename=about_helping.

Depression-Guide.com, "Depression," www.depression-guide .com/depression-definition.htm.

HealingWell.com, "Depression." www.healingwell.com/depres sion.

HelpGuide.org, "Teen Depression: A Guide for Parents and Teachers." www.helpguide.org/mental/depression_teen.htm.

Mayo Clinic, "Depression (Major Depression)," Mayoclinic .com. www.mayoclinic.com/health/depression/DS00175.

National Institute of Mental Health, "Depression." www.nimh .nih.gov/health/publications/depression/complete-index.shtml.

Gordon Parker, "Is Depression Overdiagnosed? Yes," *BMJ*, August 18, 2007. www.bmj.com/cgi/content/full/335/7615/328.

Psychology Information Online, "Depression." www.psychology info.com/depression.

Index

Picture Credits

About the Author

Lydia D. Bjornlund is a writer in northern Virginia, where she lives with her husband, Gerry Hoetmer, and their wonderful children, Jake and Sophia. She has written more than a dozen nonfiction books for children, mostly on American history and health-related topics. She also writes books and training materials for adults on issues related to land conservation, the environment, and public management. Lydia holds a master's degree in education from Harvard University and a bachelor's degree from Williams College.